IMMIGRANT

IMMIGRANT

A MEMOIR ACROSS THE ATLANTIC

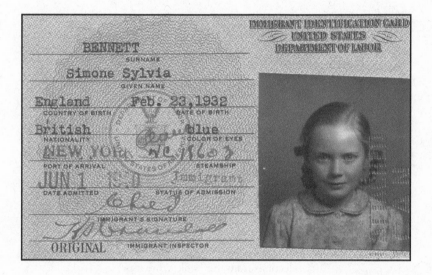

by Sally Bennett

PROSPECTA PRESS

Copyright © Sally Bennett 2013

For information about permission to reproduce
selections from this book, write to:

PROSPECTA PRESS
P. O. Box 3131
Westport, CT 06880
www.prospectapress.com

Book and cover design by Barbara Aronica-Buck

Paperback ISBN: 978-1-935212-66-9
E-book ISBN: 978-1-935212-67-6

This book is dedicated to my husband,
Marshall H. Segall,
with love and appreciation for his support
during its long gestation,
and to my children, Edward Bennett Wilson
and Diane Olivia Block,
with my love and admiration.

CONTENTS

CHAPTER 1

1932: Yorkshire

Sally, 2 years old

In my earliest photograph, which precedes memory, I am perhaps two years old, wearing a bonnet with an embroidered ruffle to keep the sun off my face, sitting in a pram looking up at someone. The expression on my face is one my sister says she sees to this day. Is it disapproval? Of what am I disapproving? Am I being pushed too slowly or too fast, or not at all? I recognize it as quick to judge, easily disappointed, impatient. Perhaps many of us, as children, judge our adult caretakers before we have language to express it. Perhaps we seethe with

1

Sally, 2 years old

resentment at our helplessness, able only to howl or beat our little spoon against the table. Those of us raised in the 1930s by nannies were subject to a more doctrinaire regimen than any child experiences in today's permissive environment. It shaped us and, perhaps surprisingly, came to our aid when the going got tough.

I was born in Harrogate, Yorkshire, in 1932, a little more than halfway between the end of World War I and the beginning of World War II in Europe, as a consequence of a deliberate but failed attempt by my parents to save their marriage.

Doris and Bill Bennett

It was a time of fundamental social change that, like the wars themselves, threw people of different backgrounds and experience together
and changed their lives in ways not previously thought possible.

My mother and father, both solidly English and descended from
the various European tribes that ranged over Europe, had grown up
close to each other in middle-class families profiting from the indus-
trialism of the 18th and 19th centuries. Both had lost sons to the First
World War, which my father, William Deverell Bennett, survived.

He and my mother, Doris Sylvia Pynegar, were married in 1918 in Catford, Kent. The Pynegars had settled around Heanor in Derbyshire, where most of them worked in the coal mines. Henry Pynegar, my grandfather, married Jane Coulter, also of Heanor, in 1881, and by 1901 they were living near London in Beckenham, Kent, and had produced 12 children. Henry is listed in the 1901 census as an electrical engineer and, besides their children, two relatives lived in the house as servants. By 1901, two of the children had died, one aged five and one less than a year old. My mother, Doris Sylvia, and her twin, Rex, were born in 1891.

The Bennetts were French Huguenots who fled persecution and settled in Gloucestershire to work in the cloth mills of the 18th century. Some became accomplished indigo dyers. Later, the family was moved to Yorkshire in a "carrier cart" to work for Billy Sheepshanks, who started the cloth industry near Leeds. Billy Sheepshanks was a well-known and wealthy industrialist who became interested in art. His collection of paintings now hangs in The Victoria & Albert Museum in London.

As a girl, my paternal grandmother, Annie Lister, was sent to Germany to learn how to use the new machines, which eventually put many of the English workers out of business. The German machines were faster and more efficient, outpacing their slower English counterparts.

Eventually, both Pynegars and Bennetts moved closer to London for business reasons, and the children grew up together. Two from each family married each other; both marriages ultimately failed. The temperaments of the two families were fundamentally incompatible, according to my mother. She described her brothers, of whom she had seven, as high-spirited, with a keen sense of humor they got from their mother, Jane Coulter. The Bennetts, on the other hand, were quieter and more serious. My mother's and father's temperaments represented their families: my mother was a romantic adventurer, whereas my father was a gentle man interested in gardening and books. My brother once asked the rhetorical question: how could those two ever have married? The answer, as trite as it seems, is that they lived next to each other. You marry people you know, especially before travel and long distance communication made other choices possible.

When I was two, my mother and father divorced and my mother married an American, Jack Cooley Pratt, and took me to live with them, first in Spain and then in Portugal. This loss of my family of origin, especially my father and brother, has remained with me. I understand the immigrant's seemingly perverse longing for a place called home, a siren song that often precludes creating a happier life in new surroundings. The familiar voices, customs, and landscape set down in infancy seem normal and right. Whatever comes later, after language allows us to shape our world, determines the course of our lives, but our emotions are forever washed in these earliest impressions.

I have often wondered what I would have become had I stayed with my father and brother in Yorkshire when my mother left to marry Jack Pratt. By her own account, she was not a very maternal woman and might not have suffered from being separated from her infant daughter. I had an English nanny, trained to care for the young, who lived with us. My father bought a large old Georgian house outside Leeds, where he had moved to become one of the directors of the Forgrove Machinery Works, which made candy wrappers. I would have been well cared for and been able to grow up with my older brother, who was sent away to school (like all middle- and upper-class boys of the time) but who lived with his father during the holidays. This has been my dream of a twin life: a life imagined but unlived, lost in infancy.

This alternative would, of course, have been impossible. It was one thing—unusual as it was—for a wife to leave her husband just because she preferred another man, but quite another to leave behind a baby. So off we went with the American: my mother, me, and my English nanny.

Jack, an engineer and colleague of my father's, already had a wife and daughter. His first wife, named Elsa, was Swiss. Together, they had a daughter named Betty. He told my mother he was divorced, but that was wishful thinking on his part when they met. Later, after Jack and my mother married, she must have learned the details of his daughter and his mother, June, who seemed to support his daughter and perhaps his first wife. Betty visited us in Portugal when she was a young girl at least once, as there is photographic evidence of her visit. My mother told me that she had suggested Betty live with us, but this offer was refused by Jack.

My mother, born in 1891, was already more than 40 years old in 1934 when she left her husband, her son, her family, and her country to marry a stranger and live in Spain.

CHAPTER 2
1933-1940: Spain, Portugal

Sylvia, Nanny, and Sally, Barcelona c. 1934–5

After their marriage in London, Jack, Sylvia, Nanny, and I moved to a flat at 198 *Calle Majorca* in Barcelona.

Barcelona was the center of Catalonia, an ancient kingdom with its own language, which had been given the right by the central government to use its language and retain certain traditional customs. After the Catalan separatists refused to support the Nationalist Party, headed by the dictator Francisco Franco, these rights were revoked. Catalonia joined the Republicans, and Barcelona was one of the first cities to fall to the Nationalists during the Spanish Civil War, which began in 1936.

Living the life of expatriates with American dollars, we had no shortage of food or any luxuries, but the streets of Barcelona were full of the poor, as well as refugees from the Russian revolution. Many former aristocrats were looking for work as maids—or anything that would pay enough to buy food. Barcelona is cold in the winter, and there was little food or fuel. Years later, my mother remembered pregnant women and small children who were starving and freezing on the streets. It is said that Franco particularly hated the Catalonians because of their bitter opposition to him and his regime.

One day, my mother went out to do an errand or take a walk and saw a man step into the street ahead of her, raise a gun, and shoot another man walking a short distance ahead. Shortly afterwards, in 1935, Jack was relocated by his company from Spain to Portugal.

Portugal was quieter, less developed, and poorer than Spain. However, Lisbon was an international city, proud of its seafaring and aristocratic history. Estoril, a seaside resort, was a short train ride down the coast. It had a gambling casino and a long beach with soft white sand. Here the monarchs of Europe, both legitimate and deposed, along with the famous and wealthy, entertained themselves during the war.

The rest of the country had not changed much in centuries. On the roads, donkeys still pulled carts or carried baskets laden with all manner of grain, vegetables, chickens, and household goods.

Ingersoll-Rand was one of the many European and American companies whose employees lived comfortable lives in countries poorer than their own. Estoril had luxury shops filled with foreign products. The hotels and casino catered to expatriates prior to and during World War II. Portuguese workers supplied their labor, learned to cook their food and care for their children, but otherwise lived separate lives.

Our family, including my English nanny, moved to a small town not far from Estoril called Paço D'Arcos. We lived in a spacious house surrounded by a park. There were maids and a gardener. My mother, now 44 years old, was pregnant with her third and last child. She had believed she was too old to become pregnant and had not bothered with precautions. This carelessness produced a 10-pound girl she called Janine.

My earliest memory is of standing in a sunlit hall outside my bedroom, with its bed full of dolls and a verandah overlooking the garden. The day is already hot in the October sunshine. I am four years and eight months old and do not know that in my parent's bedroom my mother is giving birth. From where I stand, it seems a long way to the open door. Women are moving about in the room. The one in a starched cap and apron leaves the room and closes the door behind her. She pays no attention to me.

Usually, Nanny gets me up in the morning. After washing and dressing me, we have breakfast together at a little table in my room. This morning, no one is there. Where is Nanny, Mummy, or Daddy?

Daddy appears and kneels down beside me. I cling to him. His cheek is scratchy, and he smells of tobacco, not soap. "Get dressed," he tells me. "I am going to take you to Jennifer's house to play."

Jennifer was having breakfast when we arrived: hot milk and porridge, which tasted different from Nanny's. Jennifer got white sugar to put on it while we always had brown and then Jennifer ate a boiled egg because her Mummy said she needed the vitamins. Jennifer was very thin. I did not want an egg; eggs were for lunch.

Jennifer's nurse was Portuguese. She combed and plaited my hair and washed my face while Jennifer ate her egg. I cried when she pulled my hair over my ears instead of behind them. It felt funny. I was lonely and frightened that something had happened to Mummy. Jennifer's nurse hugged me, saying things in Portuguese, but she smelled strange, not starchy and clean like Nanny or perfumy like Mummy. But soon Jennifer got out her dolls and we started a game and I forgot to be unhappy.

Daddy did not come for me until after supper. When we got home, we went to see Mummy, who was lying in her big bed, looking sleepy, with a bundle beside her. Nanny was there too. I hugged Nanny and cried a little because I was so glad to see her. Then she took the baby from Mummy's bed and showed her to me. She was very small with dark hair and eyes and tiny fingers, the size of my doll's fingers. When she yawned I laughed, and she started to cry and had to be given back.

When my sister was born, Nanny informed my parents that she would need an under-nanny to wash the baby's diapers and do other menial chores required for a newborn. This was standard practice in England where being a nanny was a professional job with certain rules, one of which was that, when a second child arrived, Nanny got a helper. This was, of course, news to Jack who knew nothing about the rules of being an English nanny.

He had hired two maids to cook and do housework. They could wash the diapers along with everything else. Two children to care for did not seem beyond one woman's ability—mothers did it all the time. But Nanny stood firm and soon was on her way back to England and we were looking for a replacement. This time, Jack hired a German *Fraulein,* a young woman to teach us German as well as care for us. He admired the Germans for their industrial and cultural superiority. We called her "Fraulein."

I have no memory of my first Nanny, who had been my primary caretaker since I was born, and I don't know whether I liked the young Fraulein. In photographs, she looks kind and pleasant, and my sister and I appear healthily disheveled from play and the sun. I never seemed to smile in photographs, while my sister can't seem to stop. In one photograph the three of us are dressed in traditional Portuguese dress, worn at that time on feast days or weddings. As she spoke no English, we spoke German together. My memory of that language, like my mother's marriage to Jack, did not survive the war.

We were pampered in ways we could not have afforded in England. My bed was covered with the dolls I loved. Once, Daddy took my favorite doll, whose porcelain head had broken, to the doll clinic in Lisbon for repair. For weeks, I waited every day for him to bring her

Mont'Alegre, Estoril c. 1939

home after work. One day, she was ready. When I opened the box, her head had been replaced by another, making her someone else, not the doll I had loved. I thought she had died and someone else had taken her place. She had been a real person to me and now she was a stranger. I felt very sad and angry.

Shortly after my sister was born, Sylvia and Jack built their own house on a hill above the casino in Estoril. They called it Mont'Alegre, happy mount. Even though Jack said he despised America, that it was a "country of back porches," his new house had all the latest American conveniences. We had central heating, a large American refrigerator, a large hot water boiler, and two full bathrooms. The good-sized kitchen, with a gas stove, was next to the dining room and large living room, which my mother called the drawing room, and the patio.

Upstairs there was a master suite with bedroom, dressing room, bathroom, and verandah, as well as three other small bedrooms and a bathroom. My sister and I shared one of the bedrooms, with a small window that looked into the room next to it. This was so Fraulein could see into the room without disturbing us.

In the mornings, I climbed into bed with my mother while Daddy dressed for work and she had her morning tea. In their large, sunny bedroom, I watched Daddy walk back and forth between his dressing room and the bedroom, partially dressed in his shirt and undershorts. He had joined the American Army during the First World War and been injured during training exercises, spending most of the war in a hospital. This left an impressive scar on his stomach, which looked like a map, the lines all running toward the center. A map, we learned later, of his personality.

My parents liked entertaining at home when they were not out dining with friends at the casino. My mother had a long white dress

Fraulein, Janine, and Sally. Estoril

Adelia, Sally, and Eduarda. Estoril

covered with blue butterflies. Can I have it when I grow up? I asked.
Behind her was her handsome husband. They were happy. I wanted
to be grown up.

Besides our family and Fraulein, we had a cook, Eduarda, and
Adelia, the housemaid. Eduarda made her own potato chips for serving
with "Gin and It"—gin and Italian vermouth—the cocktail of choice.
Early in the day, she had stopped the herdsman with his flock of turkeys
to feel their breasts and thighs looking for the plumpest. She carried it
to the kitchen, asked my mother for a small glass of brandy, which she
poured down its throat—to sweeten the meat, she said—before wring-
ing its neck. Then it was plucked and placed in a cool spot to wait for
evening. Once, a dog ran off with the turkey. Eduarda gave chase and
recovered a portion of the carcass. By this time, it was late in the day:
the guests were imminent. Eduarda purchased a second bird somehow,
repeated the preparations, and got it into the oven in time to present it
at table on time. My mother, so the story goes, only knew of this caper
because she spotted half the turkey carcass the next day.

Jack and Sylvia must have been happy with their new house and
their active social life with the other expatriates, living a version of the
colonial life away from home, where money went further and there
was a supply of cheap labor, sunshine, civilized diversions, and no taxes.

My mother was certainly happy. She had found the life for her, outside of England in the sun with a man she loved and two of her children.
If she missed my brother she never spoke of it. She always dismissed
my later questions by saying that he was away in school. Perhaps she
thought that leaving him and also the church, an important part of her
youth from which as a divorceé she was now excluded, was a bargain
struck. Stoicism was a strong value among my mother's generation—
for women as well as men. She did not look back and did not complain,
even afterwards, when the happy times were over and she had been
abandoned by the man for whom she had left family and country. She
always said she would not change anything. I believed her.

When I was about six years old, my mother and Daddy must have
decided I should go to school, but I was shy and resisted being sent to
the British school in the nearby town of *Carcavellos*. Instead, it was
decided I should have lessons with an Englishwoman and former
teacher, Mrs. Rebecca Bucknall, whose daughter, Henrietta, was my
age. Henrietta had colitis and was considered too frail to go to the
British school. My parents could not have known they were sending
me into a kind of snake pit.

Lessons were benign; Mrs. Bucknall was a kind and careful teacher.
But Henrietta, the only child born to older parents, had a terrible temper. Because of her colitis, she was forbidden certain foods—fresh fruit,
for one, which she stole from the fruit bowl in the dining room. We
ate the cherries and threw the pits under the sideboard. If she was
rebuked or refused anything, she was seized by an uncontrollable rage.

At these times, her mother would forcibly restrain her and lock her in her room. My friend's violence, the physical struggle, her screams and battering on the door terrified me. When this happened, I was sent home with a note that said Henrietta had become ill. No one ever explained, and each day began as if it would be a normal day, which it was, until one day Henrietta would again lose her temper, and there would be the struggle between mother and daughter that always ended in Henrietta being forcibly locked in her room, screaming and battering on the door.

Most days, after lessons were over, we played with our dolls. They were the babies we dressed and took out under the trees in the garden and the fields nearby. Fairies were as real to us as the rest of nature. Many children's books contained stories of fairies, and so the fact that we could not see them made no difference. We had documented proof of their existence (if we ever needed it), and why should we have thought they were less real than uncles or grandparents we never saw, or the God and Jesus Christ we sang about each Sunday morning at the Anglican Mission?

This was one of the worlds I inhabited as a child—the non-adult one, ruled entirely by our imagination. In this world, Henrietta and I were absorbed and happy. I don't remember any quarrels and certainly she never showed any of the anger that was part of the world inside the house. Outdoors was a place of liberation, indoors a place of rules.

When we left for America, Henrietta, who was good at drawing, gave me a picture she had made of two fairies, one standing on the shore, the other flying away to America. I was eight years old, and it was the end of my European life. We returned briefly after the war, but by that time I had become an American.

CHAPTER 3

Flight

I was eight in June 1940 when my mother, stepfather, sister, and I stood looking at the silver Pan American clipper ship rocking gently on its pontoons in the Lisbon harbor. The day had started very early when Mummy woke us to get washed and dressed. Until two months ago, Fraulein had been there in the morning to help us wash and to brush out our hair. She had been ordered back to Germany by her government. Janine and I both wore two long braids hanging over our shoulders. Mummy was not used to plaiting our hair and did it more slowly and gently than Fraulein who used to sometimes pull it too tight. I liked having Mummy braid my hair and wash my face. But when Fraulein left, we all cried. Nothing was the same after that.

It's only for a few months, Daddy had said. The war won't last long. We knew Daddy was staying behind, that he was not going with us on the airplane, but he did not actually say that. We were to fly in this new luxury plane, the first to cross the Atlantic virtually nonstop, putting down briefly in the Azores to refuel. We did not stop at Ellis Island but flew directly into New York City. Even so, we became immigrants, joining the vast number of people displaced during World War II.

On the dock, there were lots of people waiting to board the clipper ship. Some of them were hugging and crying. I remember it was sunny and very hot. Daddy had pushed his hat back on his head. Janine was clutching her white stuffed monkey, Tishi, a present from her Granny in England. Mummy was wearing her Persian lamb coat even though it was so hot. If we hadn't been going to America, we would be going to the beach to swim and build sand castles until it was time to go home for lunch.

After we were all strapped into our seats, the plane roared and sped over the water, then lifted up into the air. I had never felt anything like it except when I used to lie in bed and press the bottom of my tummy. This felt like that, but very sudden and deep. I loved it until suddenly my ears began to hurt a lot, and then I couldn't hear anything anymore. When I began to cry, someone gave me some chewing gum which I was never allowed to have, but Mummy said it was all right. It tasted strong and rubbery, and I still couldn't hear anything, which was worse than the pain.

Later, we all went to sleep in little beds with net bags for our clothes. The roar of the engines put me to sleep even though my ears still hurt and I couldn't hear anything. The next morning, we landed in The Azores, a place with lots of flowers. When I climbed down the gangplank, my legs felt wobbly and my head light from the roaring of the engine. It was sunny and very hot, and Mummy took off her fur coat and hat, and the three of us stood in the shade while the plane was being refueled.

Mummy said that Mr. and Mrs. Green, friends of Daddy's from work, were going to meet us in New York. When the plane took off again, I felt the same wonderful feeling in my tummy and this time, my ears did not hurt so much.

New York was very hot but gray and black, and there were no flowers. We drove off in a car over a long bridge, into a city with very tall buildings. One had a huge picture of a man blowing real smoke rings. Everything was noisy. We finally got to a gray house where the cat had just had kittens. I had never seen newborn kittens before; at home we had Blackie, a cocker spaniel, but no cats. Now Blackie was living with Hamish and his family across the street. I put my finger in one of the

Sally in New York

tiny open mouths. The kitten immediately started to suck. I liked feeling that wet little mouth tugging at my finger.

Before we left New York, our hosts took us to see the new musical *Oklahoma!* by Rogers and Hammerstein. We sat in the balcony. I remember being thrilled and awed, having never been in a large theater or to anything remotely like this.

Before we left New York, I was taken to a doctor because of my earaches. He said I had to have my tonsils out: they were infected. I remember the operating room, with the nurses and doctors wearing masks. When the oxygen mask was placed on my face, I struggled and began to scream. I saw my mother somewhere nearby, but she could not get to me. Then I lost consciousness. When I awoke, I was in bed, and my throat hurt terribly. They had promised me ice cream, but it was summer and by the time the ice cream reached me it had melted. I was bitterly disappointed.

After I recovered, we took a train to New Hampshire to stay with

Daddy's mother. She lived in the country in a large house called Sunnytop. At the station, we were met by a woman with short white hair. She said we were to call her June, not Granny. She didn't seem like a grandmother.

June drove us to a large sprawling house surrounded by grass and flower beds. It looked peaceful and safe. She took us into the kitchen, a large bright room with a modern stove and refrigerator and a table with six chairs. There were braided rugs on the floor and curtains on the windows. Through the window, I could see a cow and yellow buttercups in the field. There were two cats sleeping on the porch, and I heard a dog barking. I had never seen a kitchen like this. Ours was dark, with cupboards and a black stove. No one except the maids ever ate there.

June asked Mummy what we would like and Mummy said tea please, and milk for the children. June opened the refrigerator and took out a bottle of milk and poured two glasses. We had never been given cold milk before.

Janine, Sylvia, and Sally in New York

June told us Americans like cold milk. She put a large bowl of blue-berries on the table for us. Both tasted cold and sour. I put down the milk and looked at Mummy, who was drinking her tea with her eyes closed. I had hoped Betty would be there, but June said she was away in boarding school and wouldn't be home until her next holiday. There was a Jersey cow named Betty. June said the cow came with its name and had nothing to do with the other Betty, her granddaughter.

June had run a successful business in the garment industry as a young woman after she left Oklahoma and Jack's father. In middle age, she married a wealthy businessman, Barney Mulaney, and bought Sun-nytop when they retired to New Hampshire. She was an unusual woman for that time, even for an American. She was strong, outspo-ken, independent, and a bully. She must have thought both Jack's wives were helpless creatures who could not take care of themselves or their children. She did not have much confidence in her son, either, so took it on herself to step in and do what she thought needed to be done.

She did a lot of harm to those she set out to help—like Betty, Jack's first child. We were the second family he abandoned, but because one of us, my sister Janine, was Jack's child, June came to our rescue twice, both times with strings attached.

Mummy, of course, detested her mother-in-law, who reminded her of those gum-chewing American women she had known in Europe, with the harsh accents and common manners. (Why do they have to put down their knives to eat with their forks?) The two of them clashed almost as soon as we arrived at Sunnytop. It must have been desperation that caused Jack to send his wife and two children to stay with his mother. But it was a desperate time, with not many alterna-tives. We could not to go England, which was under siege. Portugal was full of refugees with nowhere to go, no money, and no valid papers. My mother and I had British passports and would have been deported, probably to a concentration camp, if the Germans marched into Por-tugal, which was expected. We were the lucky ones. We escaped.

But once in the safety of America, not yet at war, on a farm in rural New Hampshire, the inevitable clash of personalities occurred. The war was not going well for the Allies; the Germans were bombing England and marching through Europe. Mummy listened to all the news broadcasts. She had letters from her husband, delivered via the Ingersoll-Rand Company, which said he was well and doing important work. He didn't elaborate and didn't mention when he would come to join us in America. Mummy was sure he was working for the Allies, doing his bit for the war effort.

June did not seem impressed, and then one day she more or less admitted she was not entirely sympathetic to England and thought America would be mad to even consider entering the war. What quarrel did we have with Germany, after all? Mummy tightened her lips and said America was supposed to represent the free and the brave, and wasn't Germany trying to enslave the rest of Europe? Romantic twaddle, was June's response. German culture didn't just represent but *was* the best.

One night after Janine and I were in bed, I was woken by the sound of angry voices. I heard someone thumping the table and my mother shouting that June was a fascist and that she wouldn't spend another night in her house. Then Mummy came upstairs, woke us up, and told us to get dressed; we were leaving. An hour later, the three of us were in a taxi with badly packed suitcases, going who knew where.

June stood by the door as we left. "You're a fool," she said to Mummy. "Where do you think you are going with those children? You'll be back in an hour."

"Not by the hair of my chinny-chin-chin," said Mummy. I had not heard Mummy sound so happy since we left Portugal. I looked through the taxi window at Sunnytop. I hadn't often seen it at night, and tonight there was enough of a moon to see by. It looked like a real home. One of the cats appeared in the driveway and started washing itself. Suddenly, I was afraid. "Mummy," I said, "let's stay. Please." But the taxi had started, and no one heard me. We set off down the drive-way and soon turned into the road, and the house disappeared into the dark.

CHAPTER 4

1940: America

"What a relief!" said Mummy. As the taxi wound through the winding country roads in the summer moonlight, she explained why we had left Sunnytop and how lucky we were to be getting further and further away from that devil. The driver was sympathetic. Apparently he also had a wicked mother-in-law who deserved to be punished at least as severely as June. "She should not be allowed to have that child, Betty," Mummy was saying. "No wonder she always seemed so unhappy. When we get home, I will insist on sending for her."

The driver nodded sympathetically. "Where to, Ma'am?"

Mummy had no idea, of course, so the driver took us to a small hotel near the train station. The proprietor had to be woken up, but when he saw the three of us with our suitcases covered with international labels and heard Mummy's British accent, he closed the window and soon appeared at the door in his bathrobe.

"You refugees?" he asked, staring at the three of us standing by the taxi in our European clothes. Janine and I were wearing dresses made of Liberty cotton with smocked bodices—the first things we had found to put on—and Mummy was carrying her Persian lamb coat.

Mummy hesitated. "Yes," she said after a minute. "We're here because of the war."

He looked at their suitcases. The stickers said Pan-American Clipper Lisbon-New York.

"Lisbon"? He looked at the cabdriver as if he could explain.

"My husband is American," said Mummy. "He's still in Portugal."

The landlord was uncomfortable. "Have you got money?" he asked finally.

"I have traveler's checks," said Mummy. "We only want to stay a night. Tomorrow we are going to New York."

I could hear a note of contempt in my mother's voice. She was not used to being treated with suspicion.

Finally, he took the traveler's check and put it in the safe before showing us to a room with three beds.

The next morning Mummy sent a telegram to Jack and one to Tom Green in New York. Tom called back and advised—*insisted*, Mummy said angrily—that they return to Sunnytop, at least until Jack could advise them what to do.

"Never," said Mummy. "We'll stay somewhere near New York City until Jack comes for us. He'll be here soon."

"I'm not sure you can count on that," said Tom. "There's a war on, you know."

"Thank you, Tom," said Mummy. "But I won't return to Sunny-top."

The landlord finally decided we were bona fide refugees and offered to help us find an apartment near the City. He had a friend in Jackson Heights who found us a place in a large apartment complex that was clean and safe, with apartments to rent by the month.

Mummy thanked the landlord and insisted on leaving a large tip to punish him a little for his initial suspicions. He seemed surprised, but did not give it back.

Meanwhile, the Northeast was suddenly struck by a heat wave. Temperatures stayed in the 90s, the sun blazed every day, and no one was predicting relief.

We arrived in Jackson Heights by taxi because Mummy could not cope with the local train and the suitcases. Fortunately, there was an apartment waiting on the fifth floor: one bedroom with a pull-out Murphy bed in the living room, plus a small kitchen and bathroom.

"Perfect," said Mummy, without even asking the rent. We only had $50 left in traveler's checks and still no word from Jack. "Would you call Mr. Green for me?" she asked the manager. "I have to tell him where to forward my mail." She now believed the telephone was the way to send messages in America.

"There's public phones outside, lady," said the manager, shifting his cigar to the other side of his mouth.

"But I don't know how to use it." Mummy sounded puzzled as if she had been asked to operate a complicated machine. The three of us were standing in the doorway of the manager's apartment. The heat was unbearable, and the smell of cooked cabbage was very strong. I held my breath, something I had just started doing without realizing it. Mummy hardly looked like herself with her hair beginning to come down and her blouse sticking to her back.

The manager's wife came in to see why the door was open. "Come and sit in front of the fan," she said, "while Pete calls your friend. My grandmother was English—from London. You sound just like her."

Mummy sank down and put her head back. "I don't suppose you'd have a cup of tea?" she asked.

"Hot tea in this weather?"

"Yes, please," said Mummy.

The three of us huddled in front of the fan. It was bliss. I began to look around. The room was tiny, with a sofa and two chairs crowded together. There were piles of clothes on the chairs. Through the doorway, I could see the manager holding a telephone in his hand. Finally, he called Mummy to the phone. She got up and found Tom Green on the line. He did not sound pleased, she told me later, that they had not followed his advice to return to Sunnytop. Jack was still not to be found, he reported. He was undoubtedly up at the mines for a few days. Mummy gave him their new address after getting it from Pete and asked if her checks could be sent right away as she was out of money. None of us pretended not to listen.

Then, for a while, Mummy didn't say anything. "What do you want me to do in the meanwhile?" she finally asked. "I can't expect this kind man, Mr. Pete, and his wife to take us in free of charge." She looked up at Pete. He stared back. Mrs. Pete had gone into the kitchen. I thought she was nice and hoped she would come back soon.

After some more back and forth about calling June (Mummy refused) and reissuing checks, she hung up. They all looked at her. "Tom is going to send a bank draft while he straightens things out." Mummy looked like she might cry.

I had never seen my mother cry. What would happen next?

"Now, don't you worry," said Mr. Pete, when he heard the words 'bank draft.' "You just make yourself comfortable upstairs, and we'll hold off on the rent until your check comes."

Mummy looked up at him with what I later called her grateful-victim look. "Thank you. What would I have done without your kindness?"

Janine and I were eating our first peanut butter and jelly sandwiches and found we could not open our mouths. After a minute, we began to giggle, and then I could not control myself. The tension of the last three days turned to hysteria, and we held onto each other, peanut butter and jelly oozing down our chins.

Finally, Mummy said in her sternest voice. "Stop it this minute," and pulled us apart. She found a lace handkerchief in her bag and tried to wipe us off. Mrs. Pete went for a dishcloth and cleaned us up in no time. Then we went upstairs, carrying borrowed sheets and towels.

We made the beds, a little frightened when the Murphy swung down from the wall with a sigh at being disturbed. "Ugly old thing," said Mummy. "But it really is a bed."

Then we went back outside and down the block to the grocery store Mrs. Pete had told us about. "Eggs, milk, sugar, salt, bread, and tea," said Mummy. I looked around. It was a small store with old-fashioned wooden counters and shelves and a refrigerator for the meat and dairy products. There were bins of dried vegetables and grains and a few cartons of fresh greens, lettuce and oranges, lemons and bananas. In Portugal, when I had gone to the market with Adelia carrying a straw basket on her head, we had walked along the dusty road to a crossroads where vendors were selling fruits, vegetables, live chickens, and grains. Mummy had ordered European food from the grocer, who delivered boxes of biscuits, tins, bottled juice, alcohol, and other imports.

"This is like England," said Mummy to the grocer, who was adding up her bill. "It makes me feel at home." She was looking in her purse, trying to recognize the coins.

Janine put three bananas on the counter in front of her mother. We had eaten bananas at June's for the first time and she had loved them.

"The kid likes bananas," said the grocer. "What kid doesn't?"

"Are they expensive?" asked Mummy. She was counting out her money.

"Take them," said the grocer. "It's a welcome to the neighborhood."

"You're too kind," said Mummy. "Everyone is so nice." She sounded again like she might cry.

After supper, we unpacked a little and took baths. Later, we sat by one of the windows and watched heat lightning flicker over the skyline. It was still very hot, but in between far-off rumbles of thunder there was an occasional movement of air. I thought: *We are finally in America.* I didn't know what that meant, except that it was different but no longer so scary.

Our apartment block was built around a large park, available to all the residents. It was here that we spent most of our time that summer. There were trees and benches and grass to play on. I discovered other children and for the first time began to come and go on my own.

We waited for word from Jack, which finally came. He did not seem very surprised we were no longer with his mother, and told the company to send monthly checks to us at our new address. But he never appeared. We began to resign ourselves to being another wartime family whose father was away for the duration.

In September, it was time to start school. We had to go to the local primary school and register. We had no idea what grade I should be in as I had never been to a real school. Janine was put into nursery school or pre-kindergarten. The principal had taught school in New York City and was used to immigrants, but they had been mostly poor Eastern Europeans. Mummy, with her English accent and well-dressed children, was a new experience. "What are you doing in Jackson Heights?" the principal asked.

"Waiting for my husband to join us," said Mummy, as if Jackson Heights was a normal rendezvous point.

"Do you have family here?"

Mummy was used to this question by now. "No," she said firmly. "My family is all in England."

"My family was from England originally," said the principal. "It's a shame you couldn't get home in time. Still, they're evacuating children from London, so perhaps you are one of the lucky ones." She enrolled us without further questions.

Much to everyone's surprise, I took to it at once. I liked the school, the routine, the teachers, the subjects—except for arithmetic. I also won my first prize, a small black stuffed dog. We went to the World's Fair with a woman Mummy had hired to do some cleaning.

In December, we saw our first snow. We had to buy gloves and hats and galoshes and scarves. Mummy mourned this drain on our resources, since we never needed these things in the mild climate of Portugal. But I loved waking up to the white stuff swirling down past the window and piling up on the roof. I learned to make snowballs and hurl them at the other kids. Then a really bad thing happened to

Janine, Sally, and friend in Jackson Heights

me. The game was to hide when you saw someone coming and let them have it as they passed.

One very cold day, I waited until I spotted one of the neighborhood boys coming home and then threw two quick snowballs the way I had seen others do it and the way I had been pelted. One of them caught Peter above the right eye. He immediately let out a howl and clutched his head. When I saw the blood running down his face, my heart started pounding and I ran home crying. I was terrified I would be arrested.

Mummy was reading the newspaper. Her first reaction was irritation that I had done something like that. If I hadn't behaved like those American children with no manners, this would not have happened.

The next day, we bought a box of lollipops and took them to Peter, who had a cut that had needed several stitches. The snowball had

apparently contained a stone. His parents were fortunately not inclined
to call the police, as I had feared; instead, they treated it all like a joke.
Peter had a large white Band-Aid on his forehead and looked spitefully
at me when I handed him the candy. After that, we carefully avoided
each other. I felt chastened. How could I have done that?

By spring, Mummy was getting restless. Almost a year had passed
since we had left Lisbon, and Jack still said he could not leave. For the
first time in her life, Mummy had her own bank account with suffi-
cient if not lavish amounts of money being regularly deposited. She
had always practiced economy and had been putting money aside for
six months. She told Jack she could not face another New York summer and was going to take us to a more comfortable spot—the South.

She had been told that Southerners were English. The pace of life
was slower, cities were smaller, and you could have a house with a garden. Georgia was recommended, particularly Savannah. It was near
the original English settlement in Jamestown, and people were proud
of this heritage. Mummy would feel at home. Jack did not protest. He
sent money to cover the train tickets and a week in a hotel. They no
longer discussed his arrival date.

In early summer, after school was over, we said goodbye to Mr.
and Mrs. Pete, our friends at school, and the Murphy bed, and took a
train to Savannah. We went straight from the train to the Oglethorpe
Hotel in downtown Savannah. Compared to our arrival in Jackson
Heights, this move was done in style.

CHAPTER 5

1941: Savannah

I was nine when we moved to Savannah in the summer of 1941, and Janine was not yet five. Tom Green had given us the name of Maude Hayward, whose family went back to the early settlers and who was delighted to welcome an Englishwoman, a refugee from Europe married to an American. The Georgians we met from old families were very pro-British and in some cases identified more with their ancestors across the Atlantic than with the Americans who lived in the same town. We benefited from this attitude throughout our wartime stay in the South and even after the war, when we returned to settle permanently in Virginia. Unlike most immigrants or refugees who are often seen as interlopers, we were taken in as if we were family by people eager to be hospitable and helpful to an Englishwoman with two small children.

We rented a small brick house in a quiet neighborhood. Mummy bought some second-hand furniture and had drapes made for the living room and chintz bed covers and curtains for our bedrooms. She even bought a used piano on which she planned to give us lessons. We each had our own room, the larger doubling as a nursery or playroom with a table and chairs. It was here we ate our meals, not in the dining room, where Mummy entertained her friends and occasionally gave parties for some of the British soldiers stationed at the nearby Army base.

The kitchen was modern, with a refrigerator, an electric stove, and an ironing board that came out of the wall like the Murphy bed. There

Our living room in Savannah

Sally and Janine in Savannah

Sylvia and Gladys, Janine and Sally

was a screened-in porch off the living room with blinds and porch furniture. After a time it became the home of two squirrels Janine and I
rescued from a fallen chimney.

Mummy was always very good about taking in small animals, and
she could not resist the baby squirrels we brought home. Perhaps it
was the homeless aspect that made them irresistible even after they
chewed up the furniture and the blinds. One got part of his tail
chopped off as he went through the closing door and the other fell

into the sink. Mummy put some brandy on her finger for him to lick, thinking it would cure him; he promptly died.

We had a maid—Gladys—a tall, handsome black woman—who wore a black uniform, white apron, and cap and came three days a week to clean and wash and iron. I liked to sit in the kitchen while she ironed and listen to Gene Autry on the radio. I remember her only from photographs in which she looks like a woman of dignity and intelligence. When we left she went to work for a hotel, which in those days was a step up to better wages and working conditions.

Mummy found a community of women who played bridge and lunched together. Some had husbands, some were widows. She became a kind of star of the group, being a genuine Englishwoman, not merely a descendent, and exotic for having lived on the continent with her second husband. It was here that she forged her identity as an expatriate—never giving up her Englishness, yet never becoming an American. "Of course, I am an outsider…," she would preface any opinion on local matters. She liked life in Savannah and shared the colonial, paternalistic attitudes of her friends. Had things turned out differently, she could have lived there comfortably for the rest of her life.

I was getting older and beginning to forge a new identity, that of an American. Janine and I went to Pape School, a small private school, which generously forgave the tuition as a gesture of good will toward an ally.

I did not like school much and learned what it was to be excluded. In fifth grade, I was shy and got teased because of my accent and my European clothes. We wore the clothes we brought with us and some of them were nothing like those worn by the other students. We had velvet dresses with lace collars, which had been made for us before we left Portugal. After we had studio photographs taken in these dresses, there was no occasion to wear them, so Mummy decided they should be worn to school in order to get some use from them before they were outgrown. That they were all wrong did not occur to her.

One day, I wore my coat all day, even when I played kickball. The gym teacher asked if I wanted to take it off. I refused. When I got home, the dress was as damp and slick as a wet cat.

"What happened to your dress?" asked my mother.

"We played kickball," I said, from under the bed covers.

Mummy had no idea what the school day was like. She left school to the school. It was not part of her world. But she must have understood something, because I have no further memories of that kind of humiliation—other kinds, yes. At this time, I stopped thinking of her as *Mummy* and started calling her *Mum* or *Mums*. To my friends, I referred to her as *my mother*. Here, I will refer to her by the name she preferred, *Sylvia*.

Jack came to visit once when we lived in Savannah. It was Christmas; we had a tree and stockings, and we all exchanged gifts. I only had money saved from my allowance but I remember buying some hairpins for my mother. Like many women, she wore her hair in a roll at the back of her head secured with hairpins. She and Jack laughed when I gave her the hairpins. Did they think I did not understand or would not be hurt? I felt the poverty of the gift, which I had thought would please her.

Though I had some friends from school, my best friends lived in my neighborhood and went to public school. I wanted to go to school with Squirt and Pest, nicknames given to Anne and Joe who lived on my block. We all met in the street after school and played Kick the Can and Jacks and mumbley peg and, on rainy days, Monopoly on Joe's side porch. Sometimes Sylvia made me take my sister, even though I thought she was too young to play our games.

While the war raged, Pearl Harbor was bombed, Europe burned, and thousands died, I played with my friends on the smooth blacktop, perfect for roller skating and hopscotch. We clustered in Joe's backyard and climbed the big mulberry tree that left purple splotches all over the ground when the berries ripened and the birds ate them. Summer evenings, we played hide and seek until the huge, pale-green Luna moths appeared and we were all called home to bed.

I loved Joe but had to share him with Anne, who had been his friend longer. She was tall for her age and had a father whose right hand was missing a finger. He was a stern man who was said to whip his children with a belt. Anne never talked of this, but Joe did, and said that he too was whipped occasionally by his father. I said I was too, which was a lie, but I didn't want to be left out.

The thought of being whipped with a belt was both exciting and disturbing. Why was he missing a finger? The thought of having a man at home who was also a disciplinarian worked on my emotions in unfamiliar ways. What would it be like? I was so attached to my mother that the thought of any competition was unbearable. That one day we would be reunited as a family seemed unreal.

In the park, the lake was shaped like a map of the United States, and under the bushes were what looked like old balloons. Joe explained these were rubbers. He said they were used for fucking, a word I did not know and he would not explain except to say it was a word you never said to anyone.

One day, I said it out loud behind Joe's house. He said stop, and I said it again, louder, and he said please stop, my mother will hear you. I said it again louder and said tell me what it means and I'll stop. I felt powerful; it was wonderful. Joe picked up a stick and drew a picture in the driveway gravel. On one side was a figure with something sticking straight out below his stomach and facing him was another figure with breasts and long hair.

I recognized the figures right away. The two of us stared at the picture without saying anything and after a little while, Joe erased it with his foot. I felt funny inside: excited but kind of scared.

Later, Anne came by my house and stood outside, calling my name. This was how we communicated with each other. You went to the door or window and said, "Yeah?"

"Can you play?"

And you went out unless you were being punished or eating dinner or doing a chore. You might go next door to Joe's house or walk down to the shopping street three blocks away, where there was a dime store we often robbed of packets of chewing gum or pieces of loose candy. If you had a nickel you could go into the ice cream store and buy one scoop of rainbow sherbet. There was an empty lot with a large tree with a long rope with a knot on the end. You had to start by holding the knot near the sidewalk, then jump onto it and swing out over the low part of the lot and back again to jump off at just the right moment. I never had the nerve but we would stand and watch mostly older boys vying with each other to swing the furthest out and closest to the tree. Once I saw a boy crash into the tree and fall off the rope. He lay there while we all stared. Finally, he got up and hobbled off.

We roamed the nearby neighborhoods, dry and dusty at the end of the hot summer. Once, we came upon a grass fire, little flames licking up the brown stubble that someone must have set to clear the lot or field. We took it upon ourselves to put it out, beating the flames with our shirts, stamping them out. We were firefighters, saving the neighborhood. It didn't take long. Then we left, our job done, not waiting around for thanks.

I was not closely supervised by my mother. We had no car and I don't remember doing things with her. She had a social life and must have assumed the neighborhood was a safe place and that we would not stray outside it.I loved the movies, especially musicals with singing and dancing. One afternoon, I went alone to see the old version of *Cat People* with Simone Simon. Perhaps I thought the movie really was about cats. But it was about a beautiful woman descended from an ancient people, half-human, half-leopard, who could change her form when emotionally or sexually aroused. By the time the movie was over, it was dark outside and I had to walk some distance home. I was terrified, seeing black leopards in every shadow. For years, I was fearful of any hint of the supernatural and would not even walk past a theater showing movies such as *Frankenstein's Monster* or *I Married a Werewolf*.

In 1943, when I was eleven, Sylvia met a woman named Jean Dayton West, who was a painter married to a military man living on the nearby Army base. My mother commissioned her to do portraits of my sister and me in oil. I wore a red dress and a gold pin my English father had given me. Janine wore a Portuguese peasant blouse. We both wore our long hair loose, falling over our shoulders: hers brown, mine blonde. Normally, we wore braids, unlike the other children, who all seemed to have shoulder-length or short hair.

Janine's portrait won a prize—it showed a smiling girl with deep dimples, holding her white stuffed monkey, Tishi. I liked her portrait better than mine, which I did not think really looked like me, but the likeness increased as I got older. The artist had anticipated something in my face that was still below the surface.

Sylvia had two portraits of herself done in charcoal: in one, which showed her from the waist up, she wore a summer dress with a scoop neck and short sleeves; the other was a three-quarter-length portrait in which she was painted turning to look over her shoulder to show off her back and her black chiffon dress.

Our mother had found a way of reassuring herself that life was fundamentally unchanged. Jean West became our family chronicler. She made a charcoal copy of a photograph of my brother, Kem, in his British Commando uniform.

Our house in Savannah was full of pictures. The portraits hung in the living room and dining room along with the photographs of Janine and me as babies, lying naked on small fluffy rugs, not bearskin but probably props at the photography studio. I must have hinted to my neighborhood friends that we had pictures of naked babies. Of course, they wanted to see. Desperately self-conscious but pleased at the attention, I ushered them in one day when my mother was out. None of them had baby pictures like these.

Sally, Sylvia, and Janine in Savannah

I was beginning to change, to have real thoughts of my own, understanding certain things like trusting some people and not others and doing things you wanted and not telling your mother all the games you couldn't describe when asked what you did with your friends. There seemed to be no words for what happened; the excitement deep inside you and knowing how you had to do something like winning at jacks or throwing the knife for mumbley peg and pretending you didn't care when you got a noogie.

Gradually, my mother began to seem more different than the outside world. Instead of her, my sister, and me being normal, suddenly it became reversed: the outside world was real, and my mother became the stranger.

These were the days when the war was going badly for the Allies and there was real fear that Hitler would win after all. Sylvia invited the young English soldiers from the nearby Army base for social evenings to boost their spirits. On these evenings, they ate and drank and danced to the music of Frank Sinatra and the big bands and Vera Lynn singing "There'll be bluebirds over the white cliffs of Dover."

"May I have this dance?" He was holding out his hand. I was only eleven, closer to his age than my mother was, but I was too shy to take hold of the rough khaki-covered arms.

When Sylvia got letters from Jack, she read some of them aloud to us. He sent photographs of himself and friends in the country, hiking or having a picnic. We studied them. He had on different clothes and didn't look quite like I remembered. In one picture, he had his arm around a woman. Sylvia stared at this one a long time.

One day, Sylvia got word from Jack to meet him in New York City. She left Janine and me for the first time with Gladys. I was frightened and woke up at night. There were lions hidden in my clothes on the bedroom chair. Sometimes, I felt brave enough to reach over and turn on the light. This made them vanish. The closet was even more dangerous. If the door was left open even a crack, whatever was inside could escape.

Sylvia took a train to New York City to meet her husband. It was their first reunion since his brief Christmas visit. Perhaps she suspected the reason for his trip. The photographs might have been his way of preparing her. Perhaps he thought they would make his task easier. He had not asked her to bring us, though until they separated four years before, in Lisbon, he had been a devoted father. I did not hear the details of this meeting for some years, but later Janine and I referred to it as some families remember a summer holiday so special it becomes an emblem.

In New York, they met at the train station. He was thinner but felt and smelled the same. He was still her husband, the man she loved. At first, she forgot all her fears. At last, he was with her again and the past four years seemed to fall away. She wanted to go back to the hotel, to be alone for a little while. But he had made a reservation for lunch.

At the restaurant, Sylvia went to the ladies' room and took off her hat and fixed her hair. She was shaking. He watched her return to the table, and she could tell he was beginning to remember. But he had already ordered lunch: oysters, then something else. Obediently, she put an oyster in her mouth. It was cold and tasted of the sea. Her teeth hit something hard. They both looked down at her hand. It was a black pearl. "Tears," said Sylvia. "Pearls are tears."

"This one looks valuable," said Jack.

After the plates were cleared, he told her about the Spanish woman. They met while they were both working for the Resistance in Spain. She had been caught by the Fascists and, being Spanish, had no protection except for her lover. He could save her by marrying her and taking her out of the country.

"Live with her," Sylvia said when he asked for a divorce. "But think of the children." She refused the divorce.

First he cried; then he resorted to threats. If she didn't agree to the divorce, he would simply disappear and leave her with nothing. Spain was far away and between them a war was going on. Sylvia needed none of that. She would have liked to spurn his money. If he preferred someone else, then good riddance. She would go home and lick her wounds in private. Fortunately, lawyers were consulted and agreements drawn up. We were to have $250 a month and the house in Portugal. In those days, $250 a month was more than adequate for three people to live on, including rent. This was to continue until my sister and I came of age or until Sylvia remarried.

But agreements—even those committed to print and signed and sealed—are only paper. After five years, Jack left Ingersoll-Rand and disappeared. Sylvia never remarried. Thus, we did our bit for the war effort, as the English like to say. We saved one Spanish spy.

I had not liked it when my mother left us to meet Jack in New York. When she returned, something was different. She sat on my bed one night before I went to sleep and told me Daddy was not going to live with us again. How wonderful! I was going to have my mother all to myself. After four years, I could hardly remember the man who had been my daddy when we lived in Portugal. But everything had changed. I knew we were not safe anymore.

I could no longer sleep through the night. I would lie in bed, feeling the panic mount inside me. "Are you there?" I called out to my mother.

"I'm here," came her voice. She was not sleeping either.

A few minutes later when the pressure became too much again: "Are you there?" She never scolded me or told me to stop, only to go to sleep.

One day a telegram arrived for my mother while we were having lunch. She opened it and began to cry. My English Granny had died. For Christmas, I asked for and received a chemistry set that I was allowed to play with only in the bathroom. I cut my finger on its sharp metal shelf. Bright red blood welled up from a thin clean slice in my finger. My head spun as I tried to get up. When I woke, my head was resting against the cool white porcelain tub. There was blood on the tile floor. For years after, I fainted at the sight of blood and later carried smelling salts in my handbag along with aspirin and cigarettes.

CHAPTER 6

1944: Savannah, Hendersonville

After the divorce, Sylvia became more and more concerned with going home. Home was Portugal: Mont'Alegre, the house she and Jack had built, which she now owned. But the war was grinding on without any end in sight. In those days before air-conditioning, Savannah was almost unbearable in the summer. It was said you could fry an egg on the sidewalk, although I never saw anyone do it. Kids don't seem to notice the heat, or at least I don't remember it. Most of the women and children on our street left town for a while to escape if only to a relative in the country. The men, of course, stayed behind sweltering in their offices, rushing away on Friday afternoons to join the family.

The main concern was polio—or infantile paralysis, as it was commonly known. Public swimming pools were closed, sometimes for most of the summer, and parents were advised to keep their children away from crowds. No one knew where the disease came from or how it spread.

We spent part of one summer at Tybee beach near Savannah and another in the mountains near Hendersonville, North Carolina. At Camp Cayuga, owned by the Episcopal Church, we rented a cottage and ate in the communal dining room. We shared a table with another family whose son was allowed to pick up his food in his hands. My mother shuddered visibly as he consumed his greasy pork chop, sucking on the bone.

The lake was considered safe for swimming and there was a barn for square dancing in the evening. I do not remember having partners, only being swung around and around in a kind of wild frenzy of music and movement.

The following year, we moved from our little suburban house in Savannah on the same block as Joe and Anne to a smaller house in Hendersonville. Perhaps Sylvia needed something to occupy her until the war was over and we could return home. Savannah must have seemed used up and depressing without the prospect of her husband and their life together.

She no longer drove a car. Jack had taught her to drive, but she gave it up after a minor fender bender with a milk truck. What would happen to the children if I was killed? she reasoned. She used to walk to the nearest grocery store—many blocks away—and come home with a paper bag on each hip. We seldom took the bus anywhere and got used to walking, often long distances. We never owned another car and so never went far from home. I never traveled as a child, I only moved.

When we left Savannah, I had promised to send Joe some real lead soldiers for his collection if I could find some. Toy soldiers were no longer made out of lead during the war and therefore difficult to come by. Who knows why we thought real lead soldiers would be available in North Carolina and not in Savannah?

I remember looking out of the back window of a car at my street, where I had played with Joe and Anne. I was ashamed or embarrassed by something; probably it had to do with Joe, but its exact nature I have forgotten. I must have tried to comfort myself that I was leaving something uncomfortable behind, therefore making our departure a good rather than a tragic event. This view of flight as a remedy stayed with me well into adulthood. For my mother, it became a way of life.

This move was the end of childhood for me, if childhood means a lack of real awareness of the adult world and the ability to exist completely in moments of active and imaginative play. I had not yet become a reader, although today I still have two books that Jack gave me one year for Christmas. I wrote the name I used then, Sally Pratt, on a book plate inside the front cover. I felt possessive of them: a small piece of him that belonged to me.

In Hendersonville, I began junior high school, where I met Connie Major, a slight, dark-haired girl with a lovely smile, who became my best friend. I still wore my hair in two long blonde braids, and in 1945 I was 13 but showed no physical signs of entering puberty. In fact, I did not menstruate until I was 15.

Sally, age 13

Janine, age 9

Connie and I lived within walking distance of each other. After school, I spent most of my time at her house. Her father was a doctor and her mother a real American housewife, like in the movies. They had a big colonial house with a large kitchen and a freezer. Her mother baked layer cakes and cut up the potatoes in small squares which she explained was the way one did it up north where they came from. Connie had an older sister who was a bobbysoxer. She and her friends wore pleated skirts and saddle shoes and listened to Frank Sinatra. They ignored us, of course, but we watched them, and our doll play was modeled on how we imagined those older girls felt and behaved.

Connie and I each had a teenage doll like the Barbies that came later. In our play the dolls were us. We inhabited them as they lived out our adolescent fantasies of boys and clothes and sex. This play was fueled by our one afternoon a week in dancing school.

I have no memory of learning to dance, only of what happened after class when we went somewhere to play spin-the-bottle. When the spinning bottle stopped, pointing toward you, you went into the closet with the spinner and kissed. I cannot think of anything that has happened since that has incited that level of excitement and dread. We loathed and loved it. There was, of course, one boy, more mature than the rest of us, who was the ringleader. He understood the game, while the rest of us knew only an incomprehensible excitement.

During this first foray into boy/girl relations, we paired up. Connie paired with Boyd who became her future husband and I with a forgotten one. The boys walked us home from school, but I left mine at the corner, terrified my mother might suspect. Why was I so secretive? My mother was not strict and never showed any signs of disapproving of boys. It was not being bad I feared but being laughed at, something more common in my memory than punishment. Children were often mocked or teased, mostly in a good-natured way but it made you feel you had done something wrong or stupid. It confused and weakened

Sally, Connie, and a friend

you—or so I felt, being sensitive and shy and always the new kid on the block trying to figure out what to do this time.

Our next-door neighbors were a widow named Mrs. Bull and her son, Bartlett. He was older than I was and never a real presence in my life. Mainly I remember Mrs. Bull because she gave me my first raw oyster. We were invited to dinner. My mother often served a half-grape-fruit for the first course, but Mrs. Bull gave us raw oysters arranged in small glass bowls. I was desperate to appear grown-up, so I put an oyster in my mouth like my mother did. I gagged. The two women laughed.

Our little house—my mother called it a cottage—was truly tiny. My sister and I had our own rooms, with our chintz bedspreads and matching curtains. Mine had blue flowers, Janine's pink. We had an ice box instead of the refrigerator we'd had in Savannah. Each week the iceman came with his horse-drawn wagon and brought in a huge block of ice that went into the top compartment of the icebox. All week it melted into a metal tray that had to be emptied. By week's end, the box was no longer very cold and the milk was unpleasantly tepid. Even though I drank hot milk when we first arrived in America, I had become a cold-milk drinker by this time and was squeamish about milk that tasted more animal-like as it warmed. The other unpleasant feature of this venerated and wholesome food was its taste of garlic in spring, when the cows browsed on the new grasses.

It was during the short time (less than two years) we lived in Hendersonville, not long before the war finally ended, that we saw our divorced daddy, Jack Pratt, for the last time. We met his bus. Sylvia gripped his hand and gave him a look of anguish I have never forgotten. He took me and my sister somewhere for ice cream, and afterwards we stopped in a drugstore to buy a present for our mother—a box of talcum powder. Years later, I wrote a poem called "Sweet Dust."

Not long after this, before the war was officially over but after the fighting in the Atlantic had stopped, Sylvia booked passage for us from

New York to Lisbon on a Portuguese freighter that had been used as a
cargo vessel or troop transport during the war and hastily refitted to
carry passengers. Although there remained unexploded depth charges
in the ocean, there must have been a demand for passage from other
refugees desperate to get home because the ship was full. We packed
up our belongings and prepared to finally return home.

CHAPTER 7

1945: The Crossing

We boarded the *Algarve* in New York Harbor in early December, 1945. It was a cold, overcast day. The ship was small and battered; it looked as though it had been through a war, which it had. We followed the porter with our luggage down into the cabins below deck. Our cabin had two bunk beds and one single cot, an old wardrobe, and a sink. There were two chamber pots under the beds. The porter stacked our trunks against the wall putting one smaller case on top of the wardrobe. Obeying directions from the freighter company, we had placed our clothes and personal items for the trip in a small suitcase. No formal attire would be expected.

A porthole gave us our only daylight, and through it we could see the ocean in its many moods—we had no idea how many there would be and what a range. I bagged the top bunk, and this set off a brief futile challenge from my sister.

"Oh, well, it's only five days," said my mother.

Upstairs in the dining room and lounge, the waiters were setting the tables for the next meal, laying crisp white cloths with folded dinner napkins and heavy cutlery, as well as assorted condiments and salt and pepper shakers. The waiters wore white uniforms and bowed as we walked through into the lounge. The bartender was opening champagne and pouring complimentary glasses.

"*Bon voyage*," he smiled as he handed my mother a glass. For us, he had lemonade, decorated with a maraschino cherry and slice of orange. We stood drinking our drinks and looking around at the other passengers. There were not many of us, and most of the others were Portuguese, or so my mother thought. I listened to the language they were speaking but could no longer understand it. I had become used to hearing only American spoken and felt a sudden surge of homesickness for Hendersonville, our little house, and my friends. My mother finished her drink and, perhaps also taken aback by hearing Portuguese again, she took our hands and we started around the deck.

We passed folded deckchairs ready to be set up for the passengers. My mother wondered if it would be warm enough. We were all dressed in heavy coats and hats; my mother was wearing her Persian lamb. I was still uneasy from my first experience of homesickness. In the frenzy of the last months, getting packed, booking passage, arranging for train tickets and baggage handling, I had lost sight of what it would mean for me to leave the country that had become our home while I had gone from childhood to adolescence.

We were returning to a previous home, which in a real sense no longer existed, as least not as it had been when we left. We were returning fatherless to a country that, although remaining neutral, had nevertheless been a participant in all the activities of the war except the fighting. Most of the Europeans who had provided much of the country's income had left, and the Portuguese themselves had undergone dramatic changes. None of this occurred to me, of course, or even to my mother. What did she think we were going back to? She clung to a life even she must have suspected had evaporated during the five years of war. All we had was a house.

We left in fog and rain that shrouded the ocean. The journey was supposed to take five days, but we bucked and rolled for 14. The sea became so rough that nothing remained on any surface. The beautifully laid tables were quickly wiped clean of their cloths, their china and glass sliding, often violently, onto the floor. At first, as if refusing to submit to the will of the ocean, the waiters picked up, washed, and reset. Soon, it was clear this was hopeless: a sudden pitch would send everything off the tables into a heap of crockery, pickles, salt, pepper, butter, all wetted down by the overturned water glasses. The rolling of the boat made it impossible to keep anything horizontal. We learned to drink our soup by holding the bowl in one hand close to our mouths and either tossing it in with a spoon or drinking it from the bowl. By the second week, nothing was put on the tables until we sat down, and then we were issued a plate and glass and cutlery. People gave up table manners and reverted to more primitive ways of protecting their food. We cradled our plates on our laps or held the plate firmly on the table encircling it with the left arm and leaning protectively over the top. The dining room took on the appearance of a school cafeteria or, I imagined, a prison.

Clothing in the 1940s was much more formal than today. To be seen in public meant, for men and boys, wearing shirts, ties, trousers, and jackets—for women, dresses, stockings, and often hats. By the end of the second week, many of us appeared in our pajamas and bathrobes. Of the perhaps twelve passengers, there were never many together in the dining room, and often there was no one.

There was no purser or doctor on board. There was one Portuguese woman, Fatima, hired to make the beds and clean the rooms, who became our nurse and caretaker. She wore slippers without heels and you could hear her approach by their slap-slap on the floor. Everyone was seasick; some recovered after a few days, some remained in their bunks the whole trip. I think my mother was one of those. But we all spent the first few days vomiting into our chamber pots or whatever pan or basin she brought us. During the first storm, our suitcase fell off the top of the wardrobe, crashing onto the floor; the other trunks fell and slid across the room, temporarily trapping us inside.

One day, an American ship appeared like a ghost out of the fog and rain to escort us the rest of the way. I stopped thinking we were going to die. Only much later did we learn about the mines and depth charges. That this voyage was undertaken at this particular time, in winter, over the weapons of war rolling at random through the ocean can only be understood by knowing that refugees are a desperate lot. They will risk anything to return home.

Finally, the voyage was over; we arrived in Lisbon shaken but alive.

CHAPTER 8

Portugal Redux

The taxi that took us from Lisbon to the hotel in Estoril could have been the same one we had taken five years earlier. When we arrived at the hotel, a light rain was falling. The air was soft and warm with the memory of flowers, very different from the cold Atlantic. Across the street, the ocean crashed against the sea wall in front of the train station. I looked up above the park to where our house was waiting in the hills beyond the old casino. The brutal ocean voyage had severed my connection to America. Happiness washed over me. We were home.

Before we could move back into our house, the keys had to be secured from the attorney and arrangements made to turn on the water, etc. Meanwhile, it was almost Christmas.

The hotel was nearly empty. It smelled musty and felt colder than outdoors as we checked in. The euphoria I had felt standing between the ocean and the park, playgrounds of my childhood, had dissolved. The dining room was dark, formal, and quiet. No one said much, and the chinking of silverware and muffled voices sounded not loud but unnaturally clear, the sound of a single stone dropped in a canyon.

The day after we arrived the rain stopped, but the wind was up and it was cold. But I was excited. The shop windows, festively decorated for Christmas, were much more interesting now that I was 13 than they had been when I was eight. I bought a small wooden box, painted with flowers and the greeting *Buon Natale*. A pair of white shoes had also caught my eye, and I proposed them as a Christmas present. Too expensive, said my mother, but she finally gave in. I must have known she could not refuse me anything within reason. Christmas had always meant presents, but this year her urgency to return home by sea in the middle of winter had swept all other considerations aside.

Our timing could not have been worse. Even on our first day back, among once-familiar surroundings, it must have occurred to Sylvia that we had carried Home with us, and that small part remaining was packed up in our suitcases and boxes, not waiting to welcome us on a hill in Estoril. However, in the first days, we were pinning our hopes on the house, Mont'Alegre—happy mount—where we believed we would find something of the life we had left behind.

I wore my new white shoes only once or twice. We had nowhere to go except our house and the roads were muddy and wet at this time of the year. Those ugly white shoes and my need for them have stayed in my memory and become emblems—pathetic stand-ins—for what they were not: father, friend, or home.

The smart shops under the arcades were unchanged but now almost empty. You could still buy embroidered table clothes from Madeira (made before the war) and tinned white asparagus and *foie gras*, but there were no people around. Elderly Portuguese women sat behind the counters, opening late and closing early. The delivery bicycle remained barely used outside the provisions store, the outdoor cafe was closed for the season. We turned to the park, holding each other's hands and trying to keep up our spirits.

"Remember how glorious it is in summer?" Sylvia said, "Roses and geraniums and water lilies in the ponds to shade the goldfish."

I remembered the nursemaids sitting together with their large wheeled prams. Being very shy, I'd had few friends. One of them had been a boy named Robin who let me help him sail his boat. We pushed and poked at it with sticks until, unexpectedly, the wind caught the sail and in one glorious rush, it headed straight for the bushes and disappeared. A gardener was found who pulled the bushes apart and dipped his net many times into the water without finding any trace of it. Robin, who had a temper, got red in the face, the nurse started shouting at the gardener in Portuguese, and I began to cry. Where had it gone? I was terrified by things that disappeared.

We had the hotel to ourselves. The desk clerk was only occasionally at his post, and the staff consisted of one chambermaid, a part-time cook, and a combination waiter and dishwasher. They made us our meals—usually something with eggs and rice. Choices were not available. On Christmas day, we had chicken and rice. Afterwards, the waiter brought us a tiny English Christmas pudding—Crosse & Blackwell's—from a tin. We had seen them in the fancy grocery story in the arcade. The cook had put a sprig of evergreen on top and doused it with brandy. Before he divided it carefully into three portions, the waiter ceremoniously put a match to it and a blue aura sprang up.

"*Buon Natale*," murmured the waiter.

"*Buon Natale*," we murmured back.

My mother looked as though she might cry as we received our small portions. My sister took a bite and immediately spit it out. "You got the lucky piece of silver," said Sylvia. She took the tiny silver ring from my sister. My mother was superstitious and all her life depended on a variety of charms designed to ward off bad luck. We turned over a piece of silver under a new moon, never opened an umbrella in the house or put a pair of shoes on the table, threw any carelessly spilled salt over our left shoulders, and embedded small silver bells, rings, four leaf clovers, and horseshoes in our Christmas pudding every year. This one came at a good time, and it lifted her spirits to think one of her children was to be happily married.

The waiter looked impressed. They both beamed at Janine, who smiled obligingly back and tried to put the ring on her finger. It was much too small.

Finally, our house was ready—cleaned, electricity and water turned

on, the beds made. The furniture was as I remembered it: the dark dining room with heavy Jacobean furniture, high-backed chairs uphol-
stered in red, the refectory table, the heavy sideboard, the chandelier
with small red lampshades on each bulb. The living room, which we
called the drawing room, had a fireplace at one end and a writing table
on which lay a soft Italian leather case tooled in gold.

This writing case stayed with my mother until the end of her life,
and I have it now, discolored and no longer soft. Like her, it endured
all the changes, bearing the marks of what it passed through. There is
a large stain from spilled ink, a hardened circle from a too-hot cup or
ashtray and numerous cigarette burns. The folder is dirty and the gold
tooling faint. It does not encourage or comfort me as do the pair of
Portuguese tiles that hang in my kitchen: in one, a baker in a straw hat
strips the grain; in the other, he wears a white apron and is removing
round, flat loaves from an oven on a wooden paddle. These are still
clean and whole, their message enduring and optimistic. The old
leather case represents something darker. It was one of my mother's
last possessions, of no value and therefore never sold. It is my *memento
mori.*

Now we could not afford the oil needed to fill the large underground tank, and so the beautiful American furnace remained unused,
a monument to someone else's dream, someone no longer present. We
used the gas stove for heat as well as cooking. Fortunately, natural gas
was not expensive although the ordinary wood or coal stove found in
most kitchens would have been more practical. The refrigerator had
its coils on the top and at times was not as cold as the outside air temperature. It did not know how to make ice. We filled the tiny cubed
trays with water and every few days I stuck my finger into one of the
cubes, hoping to find it solid. Never. In fact, the water was not as cold
as the water from the tap, which came from deep underground and
which we could not drink. Our drinking water came in large wicker-
covered demijohns, delivered once a week by a man driving a very old

truck from a bottling plant in the hills near Sintra, a nearby mountain town with a famous castle.

None of these inconveniences troubled us except for the cold. We should have waited until spring, my mother admitted, as we huddled over the gas jets in the kitchen. Still, it was never cold enough to freeze, and in the evening we spent a lot of time under our blankets.

We ordered our food from the store in Estoril. It was delivered on the same bicycle we had seen propped idly by the door. Sometimes we splurged and bought a box of Kellogg's Corn Flakes, outrageously expensive and always disappointingly soft. I can taste them still. We also bought tins of Favorita chocolate-covered biscuits and were rationed to two a day. They kept up our spirits and gave us something to look forward to. Most mornings we made porridge from Quaker Oats. Before the war, one of our maids used to shop at the outdoor market, where local foods must have been very cheap. Now it was winter, and we had to buy everything from the store in town.

In our old nursery, with the table by the window where Janine and Fraulein and I had eaten our meals, was our wind-up RCA Victrola and collection of records. Before the war, the Victrola had stood in the drawing room where Sylvia and Jack and their friends had danced to "Red Sails in the Sunset" and Nelson Eddy and Jeannette McDonald singing "The Indian Love Call." The renter, who had occupied the house during the early days of the war, must have moved it.

Now we played the Frank Sinatra recordings of "Saturday Night is the Loneliest Night of the Week" and "All of Me" that Sylvia had played for the British soldiers she had entertained in Savannah as her contribution to the war effort.

I think it rained for the first few months in Estoril, and I don't remember ever seeing another person. There were a few houses nearby, mostly built like ours by British or American expatriates, now standing empty. Only one family remained from those we had known, living in an old house further up in the hills, called Casa Senora de Fatima after the famous saint whose shrine was nearby. We were invited one day for tea by Rebecca Bucknall, my first teacher and the mother of my friend Henrietta.

An elderly Portuguese maid opened the door. The hall was as cold as all interiors were at this time of the year. She showed us into the living room, where a fire burned in the grate. The room was cozy but shabby and sparsely furnished. It all looked familiar but foreign—smaller than it should have been. Through the window, I could see the garden where Henrietta and I had played.

The door opened and in came a woman with short, straight gray hair. She smiled and held out her hand. "Mrs. Pratt," she said. "How good to see you."

My mother took Rebecca's hand but said nothing. The two women stood, hand in hand, without speaking. Janine and I watched. We were looking for clues—anything to help us understand. Then Rebecca turned toward me.

"Sally, my dear," she said. "You've grown up." She pulled me to her and hugged me.

Her heavy sweater scratched my face, and I pulled back. I did not like being hugged. Then she turned to my sister, who smiled at her, too young to be caught in the chains of memory. We finally sat down, and tea and cakes and bread and butter were brought in. We learned that Henrietta was in school in England. Rebecca's husband had died of a heart attack during the war, and she was preparing to sell her house and move back to England to be near her daughter. I wondered what Henrietta was like now and wished she were there. I gave Mrs. Bucknall the present I had bought for Henrietta, a round leather purse with her name on it. Like everything else, it seemed wrong.

CHAPTER 9

1945: Mont'Alegre

We had not been in Portugal long before I knew I wanted to go back to America, but I couldn't tell my mother. This was supposed to be home, the place where you knew what to do, where people were glad to see you because they knew you, like the girls who were glad to see their friends every morning, who whispered together in the cloakroom, made plans. Connie and I had been like that, but now Connie was there and I was here. And here wasn't home anymore.

My mother didn't like America. You could hardly blame her, considering the way my stepfather had treated her. Actually, he didn't seem to like America very much either. None of his wives had been American. His first was Swiss, his second—Sylvia—was English, and now there was this Spanish person.

"I was a fool to leave," my mother said. "He was a man who had to have a woman." This became a kind of litany, repeated over and over during her lifetime. She was right, but she had been brought up to obey and endure. Other families had stayed on and were quite safe. Portugal had remained neutral, and the Germans never came.

I was beginning to remember what it had been like before. I thought I had forgotten—I actually had forgotten—until we got there and then it all started to come back. The house and furniture were the same, but the air had changed. It used to smell good—of food and Sylvia's perfume and Jack's cigarettes. Now it just smelled cold—even when it was hot outside, when we would have got ready to go to the beach after breakfast to the smell of Eduarda's soup on the stove and clothes being ironed with the old-fashioned irons, while the two maids laughed together and men selling vegetables or sharpening knives called up from the street. Now the street was empty, and the house smelled of emptiness, of things put away, of people gone.

We lit the electric heater in our bedroom and lived there, eating from the same table we had with Fraulein before the war. Sylvia moved into the second small bedroom (once Fraulein's) giving up her own large one with the verandah. We did not use the dining room; like the drawing room, it was designed to be cool in summer and centrally heated in winter. Now both rooms seemed cavernous and uninviting. Sometimes I touched the cold radiators, imagining what it would be like if they were warm and all the doors were open and the rooms occupied.

While we made porridge in the morning, we watched the cats outside the windows. They had taken up residence in our back yard while the house was empty and, now that it was early spring, the females came into heat. At night they yowled and fought.

"They're starving," said Sylvia. She shuddered. "We can't feed them or they'll never leave."

I thought they made a lot of noise for starving animals and stared at them while waiting for the water to boil. They were all thin and some had clumps of fur, ears or eyes missing. When they weren't staring in the window, hoping for food, they were fighting, or what I thought was fighting. The females yowled when the males pinned them down, growling, their ears laid back. When they stopped pumping in and out, they grabbed the female by the back of the neck, dismounted, and then shot off into the bushes.

Although the cats repelled and frightened me, I couldn't stop watching. When Janine climbed up on a stool to see what I was looking at, I lifted her down. She didn't have to watch it. After a while the kittens began. Sometimes the mothers dropped them anywhere. One morning there were six tiny creatures, barely moving on the brick walk. Soon there seemed to be litters everywhere, most of them dead. The ants quickly began doing their work. If it didn't rain and the sun came out, the cats went off to hunt. Sylvia and I began to bury the dead kittens. Otherwise they got eaten, sometimes still alive, eyes still closed. Sylvia finally forbade me to watch. "It's disgusting," she said.

At this time, I got a letter from my father telling me he had married a woman named Barbara Batley—an old friend—and they were expecting a child. I remember reading his letter in the cold kitchen and starting to cry. We had left him, of course, but I believed he remained steadfast, living in Leyland House, waiting for the war to be over when he and I could be reunited. Now he, too, had left me for someone else.

In Daddy's old dressing room, I studied myself in the long mirror. There was almost nothing about my appearance that pleased me. My skin was too white and thin, covered with my spring crop of freckles, making me look rather sickly. I hated my freckles. Sylvia said they were the sign of a good skin but to me, they were blemishes. I knew exactly the skin I wanted; it was pale gold with no freckles. My hair was long and braided. As I studied my body in the mirror I thought of my friend Connie, who was thin and often sick. The image staring with irritation back at me was sturdy and not yet feminine except for two slight swellings on my chest. I turned away before something else happened. As desperate as I was to grow up, I did not like surprises.

I flopped down on the small chair, the only piece of furniture in the room. All our books had been stored here while the house was rented, giving the room a smell I would later recognize in libraries, of old paper and ink and dust, a smell that would bring back this safe place, where I sometimes caught the smell of Daddy's clothes although his closet was empty.

In America I had read books like *The Secret Garden, A Girl of the Limberlost*, and *Green Mansions* about girls growing up without real parents. These girls were never good. They were what Sylvia called "difficult." They sulked and talked back and aggravated whoever was taking care of them. They made friends with other misfits like Colin, the crippled boy, and the cranky old gardener, or they wanted to live in the woods and make their own shoes, or they knew the songs of the birds like Rima, the bird girl. I craved self-sufficiency.

The books I read now in this little room were very different. They were about men and women. Things happened that I did not always understand about wanting and not having. Some were stories like *The Razor's Edge*, in which a woman loved a man who was looking for God. This had a powerful effect on me and made me want to cry. I hated to cry. Others were about Mary Queen of Scots and other ladies with bodices and bosoms and men who were pirates or soldiers. They were never sad, even though a lot of terrible things happened. I began to think that being beautiful (all the ladies were beautiful) was exciting and necessary.

When I finished the novels, I read Margaret Sanger's book on birth control. This made me wonder why none of the heroines in novels ever had babies or even worried about it since it was so easy to get pregnant. It seemed unlikely they had any of the devices or methods Margaret Sanger recommended since they lived long ago. How could I trust what books said if they left out important things like that?

"None of the ladies in those books upstairs ever have babies," I told my mother one day. Usually I did not ask her about anything I suspected had to do with sex or babies because it annoyed her. On this occasion, she simply shrugged and said she supposed it was just luck. Everything seemed to come down to that, I thought, but still wondered if some books told the truth more than others.

I worked my way methodically through all the books in the dressing room. *Sight Without Glasses* told you to throw away your spectacles and do eye exercises instead. Apparently Jack had thrown away his black-rimmed ones (I tried to think of him as Jack, not Daddy any more). I read about Theosophy, which explained how we all see the world through rose-colored glasses. I knew these weren't real like the ones you could throw away: rose-colored ones made the world look prettier than it was.

I was learning that I often didn't see things the way my mother did. She said things that I thought were just silly, like when she talked about how so-and-so worshipped so-and-so. It was some time before I understood that my mother's use of language was old-fashioned; much later I liked it and sometimes adopted some of her expressions.

Sometimes on Sundays, Janine and I went to the children's movies that were shown in the afternoon at the Casino—mostly Walt Disney. We saw *Tres Amigos,* in which the rooster sang popular Spanish songs like "Granada" and "Sorrento." Sylvia had given me enough money to buy several lollipops—delicious ones with intense fruit flavors. Even I had to admit they were better than the ones in America—better even than Tootsie Pops. We were early, so we consumed our ration before the movie began. I found enough money in my pocket for one more.

"Orange," said my sister.

"No," I said. "Raspberry's better."

She actually began to cry.

"Oh, all right," I said, disgust dripping from my words and slapped the money on the counter, leaving her to get the lollipop and then rush after me into the theater. I knew how frightened she was of our getting separated. As soon as the lights went out, I sensed someone at my shoulder and suddenly a shower of lollipops poured into my lap. I was stunned. The theater was already dark and when I looked around, no one was there and the movie had begun. Janine and I stared at each other. We had very little experience with miracles.

Janine giggled. "What are we going to do," she whispered. "Can we eat them?"

I made a bowl of my skirt. There must have been several dozen. The one I picked out was raspberry; it was delicious.

One day, when the rain stopped, I was leaning on the white plaster wall of the balcony outside my mother's bedroom, looking over the trees to the sea. On the other side of the water was America. Three months ago, it had been home. Now it was a foreign country. The tiles felt cool on my bare feet, and I could smell the warm fragrance of the sweet peas that were growing wild by the road. The sunny part of the wall was very hot.

I put my cheek against the cool part of the plaster and looked across the street. Hamish used to live in that small house. Now it was empty.

I stared at the road again. Two black specks appeared, crawling up from the little railroad station. Soon, they became two women dressed in black, barefoot, carrying a bundle each. I watched them pause in front of our house, then press the buzzer on the gate. Our house was surrounded by a wall and a gate that could be opened only from the inside. This was common practice, designed as protection against beggars. Some houses had high walls, the tops covered with broken glass. I heard the buzzer ring inside the house and the answering click as my mother opened the gate. I rushed to the stairs. We never had any visitors.

"How did you know we were back?" I heard my mother ask the two women when they got to the door. They were dressed in shapeless black dresses, their hair tied neatly back; but now, hot from the long climb from the railroad station, their faces and hair were damp with perspiration. My mother looked more upset than glad to see them. Then I knew. These were our maids before the war. Eduarda, our cook, took Sylvia's hand and curtsied, then let go a flood of Portuguese. They both wanted to come back to work. Eduarda had been married, but her husband was killed in an accident. Adelia, her younger sister, who had cleaned our house, washed our sheets and clothes, and waited at table, smiled but said very little.

I understood most of what was being said, even though I couldn't actually say any Portuguese words. It was weird to remember what the words meant but not be able to think of them.

"I have no husband," Sylvia told them, "and no money to pay you. Mr. Pratt has gone away."

Hearing this news, the two women began to cry. Eduarda took Sylvia's hand and held it against her cheek. Adelia wiped her tears away with a corner of her shawl. I had hardly ever seen any grownups cry, even when we had to get into the Clipper Ship and leave Jack behind. I held my breath while they shook my mother's hand, kissed it, then picked up their shawl bundles and left. Once outside the gate, they took off their shoes, tucked them in their shawls and set off back down the road to the train station.

CHAPTER 10

The Confidant

It was at this time, when the three of us were alone in Portugal in the house my mother and Jack built, that I heard the story of my mother's life. I was young and not able to evaluate its impact except that it seemed very real to me. She was a good storyteller and, at that sad time in her life, she took comfort from remembering her youth. My imagination took hold of the story and brought the characters to life.

At the turn of the century, Doris, or "Dor" as she was known, was nine years old. It was a time of great optimism and self-assurance in England. The middle class was riding on the crest of the industrial wave. Business was good with its colonial markets overseas, and men like her father, Henry Pynegar, could afford to support a large family in very comfortable circumstances at Tamar, their house near the small village of Beckenham, from where he was driven each morning in a pony and trap to catch the train to London. Riding in an open carriage, through a still unspoiled countryside of birdsong and flowering meadow, he was sometimes mistaken for Edward VI, with his impressive figure and black beard. People bowed to him and took off their hats. Like the king, he was handsome and successful with the ladies. He also loved his wife, Jane, a beauty with sloping eyes, a fine figure, and a sense of humor.

The two younger girls, Gladys and Doris, were only a few years apart in age, and they vied for their father's favors. Who would take out the silk handkerchief and carefully wipe the dust from his top hat before he left for the station? Who would drive him? Doris, as the elder of the two, usually had the privilege. She adored Da and he favored her. She was like the boys in temperament: high spirited, independent, and impatient. Gladys was gentler, and closer to her mother.

In spring, Daisy, the pony, clip-clopped along the road between the hedgerows, startling the birds at their nest-building. Magpies lifted off as they approached, their beaks dripping with egg from a plundered nest. From the fields came the rich smell of manure.

"Mind your shoes," Mother would have cautioned the children when they came in from play. There was always one—probably the youngest boy—whose appearance was greeted with howls from one of his brothers to look at his muddy shoes, bringing Jesse, the oldest daughter, from the kitchen frowning at his language and ready to prevent the damage from penetrating further into the house.

The front door, forbidden to the children, was already scraped of its finish by Daisy who, if neglected, would somehow escape her stall and paw and stamp at the front door to get attention. This trick was, of course, wildly popular with the children, and Daddy had been known to wonder aloud how such an intelligent animal, who could let herself out of her stall at will, could not find her way back home from the neighboring village. Besides Daisy, there was Roger, the plum pudding dog, whose whip-like tail wagged with pleasure at being allowed into the drawing room.

At dinner, Father sat at one end of the dining room table, Mother at the other, and, while their father carved, the boys vied with each other for their mother's attention. She adored her sons, and they repaid her by making her laugh. Once they became prosperous, Henry indulged her with splits of champagne, and after a glass she became an even better audience, silently rolling from side to side at her sons' stories.

About 1905, Henry decided it time for a family photograph. The family awoke early to a perfect summer day. There was no time to

Standing from left: Jane Coulter Pynegar, son (?); sitting from left: son, Doris Sylvia, Henry Pyneger with a child on his lap

dawdle: baths had to be taken and hair combed, clothes had to be clean and pressed. The maids, with the help of the gardener, took the rugs and chairs outdoors.

As each child was readied, he or she was required to sit in the drawing room and wait. At last it was done. Mother and the girls wore their best frocks, with embroidered collars, full sleeves, and pieces of jewelry. Daddy and the boys wore coats and ties. The two youngest boys had short pants and blouses.

The photographer composed the group. He directed everyone where to look; some forward, some to the right and some to the left. No one smiled, the situation was too serious. Their expressions ranged from mild alarm and vigilance to contemplation.

How different they all were. Vernon and Jesse, the two oldest,

Donkey "Daisy" with child, Doris, and Gladys

stood at the top, staring into the distance like figureheads on a ship. Jesse's hair, like Mother's, was coiled on top of her head in the manner made famous by the Gibson Girls. On one side stood Kemys with his saturnine smile, then Reginald, his "north" eye hidden by the direction of his gaze. Harry's pointed ears made him look like an elf standing behind one of the seated twins. Doris stared, rapt, into the distance, her mouth slightly open. On the other side, Daddy is holding the next-to-youngest boy, Donald, and on his right sits Doris's twin, Rex. Mother was the center, with one arm around her youngest daughter, Gladys, and in her lap the baby, Sylvanus. She is staring directly into the camera, and her expression is not one of trust.

No one is over 45 years old. All are handsome and vigorous: flowers of Imperial England. Who could have guessed that within 10 years, two of the boys, including the youngest, would die in the Great War, and a few years later Doris and one of her brothers would leave the country, never to return in their parents' lifetime?

CHAPTER 11

School

Over the years of my childhood, I heard about my mother's school days. Perhaps because I did not go to a formal school until we got to America when I was eight, her memories of a girl's school in the early 19th century sounded almost romantic. Only later did I understand how harshly the girls were treated and how deprived they were of any real knowledge or intellectual training. They were taught self-discipline, respect for authority, and some social graces.

Doris and Gladys went to an expensive finishing school designed to prepare girls for life in the middle and upper class. The school was run by a Frenchwoman, known simply as Mademoiselle, and an Englishwoman, Miss Self. The school was a former manor house. The bedrooms were dormitories, and there were rooms for lessons, a dining room, lounge, kitchen, and chapel. Like all houses at this time, it had no central heating and was warmed by coal or wood fires in the main rooms. The bedrooms were unheated.

The girls were taught sewing, deportment (how to sit and walk), elocution (how to speak), French, and some literature—Milton, Shakespeare, Wordsworth, Keats—considered appropriate to the social and moral goals of the school. The girls were being prepared for marriage, for motherhood, and, most important, for positions as wives of the future leaders of the country and the empire. The comfort of the girls was not considered, any more than that of their male counterparts in the public (private) schools that shaped those future leaders.

In Britain, daylight is as short in winter as it is long in summer. At school, Doris was woken by a loud bell before it was light. She jumped out of her warm bed, shivering as soon as her feet touched the floor, and broke the ice in the basin so she could wash her face and teeth.

"Hurry up," chattered Lottie Bennett. Two of my fathers' sisters, Lottie and Dorothy, also attended this school. Doris did not like them any better than she did their brother, Bill. Since the 15 girls shared one ewer of water, the water got scummier as it was used. Doris unplaited her long braid and started brushing. This was the worst of her early morning tasks. Her hair was thick and long and her fingers were stiff from the cold. She only had a few minutes to brush it out and replait it before getting to breakfast and inspection by the head-mistress, Miss Self.

By now, the girls were all up, talking and giggling in subdued voices. They could see their breath in the dim light—little puffs of warm vapor. Doris winced as her hair caught in one of the chilblains on her knuckles. This winter was unusually cold and most of the girls had painful sores on their fingers that bled when the skin cracked. She pulled her dark brown hair tightly back from her forehead and began the long heavy plait, wishing she was one of the lucky girls born with thinner hair who could wear a fringe and tie the rest back.

The headmistress insisted on absolute plainness of appearance. No mirrors were allowed and no curls or other decoration. Obedience, modesty, and endurance were the three virtues of the Victorians, and this school was, like most institutions, a bastion of tradition, looking back for guidance, never forward.

By now, most of the girls had left the room. Doris tied the end of her plait and ran after them. She was buttoning her heavy blue serge blouse when she reached the dining room. Fortunately, Miss Self had not yet appeared. The maid was passing around the bowls of porridge and mugs of tea. Until last year, the girls had to spend the first hour of the day in chapel praying, before they were allowed breakfast, but there had been a lot of illness as well as enough complaints from parents that Miss Self had to allow breakfast first.

The door opened. A tall, thin woman entered, wearing a dark blue skirt and heavy blouse, her hair pulled back in a bun.

"Good morning, Miss Self," rang out a chorus from the table.

Miss Self seated herself at the head. "Good morning, girls." She did not smile, but looked quickly around to make sure everyone was there. One seat was empty. "Dorothy is still in the infirmary," she said, "but Sister assures me her chest is much better, and she should be back with us in a day or two."

Severe respiratory ailments were common: bronchitis, pleurisy, ear infections. Some girls became ill each winter; some had to be withdrawn from school; some died. The school was neither held responsible nor blamed.

After breakfast, the girls stood by their chairs for inspection. Miss Self toured the room, examining finger nails, hair, and necks, and noting obvious stains on clothing. Since the girls changed their underclothes only once a week and their skirts and blouses when summer came, stains were a serious matter. Miss Self looked at Doris's swollen knuckles. "Are you drying your hands well?" she asked.

"Yes, Miss Self."

"See Sister for some salve. We don't want any infections. And dry them a little better."

Doris heard Lottie Bennett snigger. Cow. Miss Self was telling Lottie to tighten her vest band. Poor Lottie had large breasts and was required to bind them inside her vest. Doris knew Lottie was jealous of her because of her clear skin and good figure. And because she could make the other girls laugh. When they were at home for holidays, the boys, especially Bill Bennett, flocked around Doris. Everyone knew he adored her but was too shy to do much about it. She was considered to have "It," or sex appeal, as it was later known, unlike the Bennett girls, who definitely did not. Doris knew she was not pretty—Jesse, her older sister, was pretty—but then again she was not boring like the Bennett girls. Doris thought Lottie was thick in every way. Dorothy, her sister, was thin, spoke very softly, and had a weak chest. She was even shyer than Billy was. Doris knew Dorothy didn't like her because Doris did not treat Billy very well.

After breakfast, they all went to chapel for an hour. By this time, the sky was getting light and the small east window of stained glass glowed red and blue and yellow. The chapel was freezing, being far away from any source of heat, and the girls were allowed to wear their coats and gloves. In spite of the cold, this was a favorite time of the day for Doris. She could stare at the window and put herself in a kind of trance in which she forgot her body and its discomfort. She felt lightheaded and pure, filled with a kind of ecstasy she assumed had something to do with God. Her body tingled and her eyes stung. She closed them and leaned her forehead on the chair in front of her. The priest intoned the matin prayers, and sometimes she slept.

Doris's best friend at school was Grace, who had thick, curly red hair no amount of plaiting or pulling back could tame. It burst out of plaits and curled around her head like a halo. She was physically robust, and even the harshness of the school could not diminish her energy. Everyone liked her, even Mademoiselle and Miss Self, who deplored her zest but could not resist it.

"Grace, compose yourself," could be heard throughout the day as she took the stairs two at a time and gulped down her tea. Her family lived near the school and visited at least once a week, taking Grace out for a meal and usually one of the other girls as well. This probably accounted for her superior health, as the meals at school were meager in quantity and quality. Lunch was usually a thin soup and then a steamed suet roll or pudding. Supper was sometimes an egg but more often sardines or potted meat on toast and a plain cake. Salads were unknown and vegetables were usually a stuffed marrow or overcooked carrots.

Everyone knew Grace was in love with Doris. Doris liked her friend but also enjoyed the power she had—laughing at Grace when she got all soppy about her. She knew Grace's feelings were different from hers, different from the usual kind of crush one girl had on another. There was something very serious and intense about Grace underneath her boisterousness. Sometimes Doris caught her staring, and then Grace turned red and her freckles stood out. Sometimes when it was very cold, after the lights were out, they got into bed together.

"I love you," Grace whispered.

"Be quiet," said Doris. She was warm for the first time that day and wanted only to go to sleep.

Doris left school around 1907 when Edward had been king for six years and the country was affluent and full of confidence. She lived at home, drove her father to the station each morning and waited for a suitable man to appear. So far, only Bill Bennett had made an offer, and she had turned him down. Her father disapproved, but she was his favorite, and he could not force her to marry someone she did not want—not yet.

The older two children, Jesse and Vern, were already married. Vern had joined his father's firm, and Jesse married Harold Pilbrow, an entrepreneur, who was making a name for himself in finance. Mother did not approve of Harold at first. His background was shadowy and his business philosophy daring—a "diamond in the rough," she called him. But he wooed Jesse vigorously, with genuine feeling. Surprisingly, Daddy was in favor of the match. Mother pointed out, tightening her mouth, that his oldest and prettiest daughter was being pursued by someone who could turn out to be a ne'er-do-well.

But Harold loved not only Jesse but also her father, whom he respected. The older man treated him as a kind of protégé. So he and Jesse were married, and Harold consulted his father-in-law in all his business dealings. Even after the war, when Henry Pynegar lost everything in the Depression, Harold continued to consult him, although he no longer always followed his advice. Eventually, he and Jesse took Henry and Jane in and cared for them until they died.

Those days before the war were happy ones for the Pynegars. The younger boys were still in school, the older ones in business. Everyone except Vern and Jesse lived at home. Neighbors visited. There were parties. Doris was now the oldest girl, and she helped her mother run the house. She made Mother's dresses by hand, carefully sewing tucks in the bodice, making the full sleeves, the snug cuffs.

When Gladys came home from school, she borrowed her older sister's things and sometimes forgot to return them. The two girls had never been good friends, and Mother usually took Gladys's part, or so it seemed to Doris. Gladys was very pretty and was having a good time with her own friends. She also had a very attentive suitor, but Mother thought she was too young to marry just yet, so she went to town with her friends and told Harry Horley he would have to wait. "You're just jealous," she taunted Doris when her sister complained of something she had done.

"Because of Harry?" Doris raised a heavy eyebrow. "Don't make me laugh." She went back to cutting up squares of cotton cloth to use for her monthly periods. She needed a lot because she bled so much and they had to be washed by hand. She tried not to go far from home at those times.

Gladys looked at the squares. She had just started menstruating at 16. "How long does it go on?" she asked.

"Forever," said Doris, "except when you're having a baby."

"Does Mother still do it?"

"Ask her," said Doris. She was still irritated at her sister for taking her stockings. She knew Gladys wouldn't ask Mother. You didn't ask your parents those kinds of questions. The only reason Doris knew her mother no longer had monthly periods was because she never saw any of these squares hanging up to dry.

CHAPTER 12

1917: England

One day, Doris went down the stairs, smiling to see Kemys and Rex lounging in the hall. They were laughing with a third man, who looked up as she approached.

"Here's Heinrich," Rex said. "He's a Mason, like Daddy, and he's going to hunt lions in Africa."

"Heinrich Heyman," the man said, bringing his heels together. "It's a pleasure."

He looked Vern's age, she thought, heavier but the same height, with dark blond curly hair and a beard. His eyes were brown and his skin tanned. His clothes were older in style than her brothers' and somewhat worn, giving him a dated, romantic look. She normally felt at ease with her brother's friends. This one was different.

For a few minutes, no one said anything. Then Kem gave his sister a poke with his elbow. "Come on, Dor," he said. "Give us a beer."

They all went into the lounge while Doris went to the cellar for the drinks. She took a large beer and a small ginger out of their cool storage and put them on a tray with glasses and a bottle opener. Who was he and where did he come from? She felt more excited than she thought she should.

As they drank their beer, Heinrich answered Kem and Rex's questions about Africa. A lot of Germans and Americans were interested in hunting game and paid high fees for being taken on a shoot.

Heinrich had been born in Tanganyika on his parents' farm, and he knew all about hunting. Later, the family moved to Kenya. He had friends among the young Masai men, each of whom had to kill a lion in order to become a man. "I'm going to start a safari club in Nairobi," he said. "I'm looking for backers."

Heinrich had spent 10 years growing coffee on the family farm, but the crops had been poor lately and he wanted to get out. "There's just enough for the parents," he said, "but not for me. Too much work and one day we'll have to get out. It's not really our land."

"You've lived there all your life," said Doris.

"I'm German," said Heinrich. "It makes a difference. But that doesn't mean I don't want to live there. It's paradise compared to this country—or anywhere."

Doris tried to remember what she knew about Africa. "Isn't it very hot?" she asked. "And dangerous?" The picture that came to mind was a large pot with steam coming out surrounded by naked black men and tigers.

Heinrich smiled. "No one here knows anything about what it's like. Nairobi is very high up and never hot. Some of the animals can be dangerous but only if they are frightened or starving. The Africans are no more dangerous than anyone else."

"Tigers?" asked Doris

"There are no tigers in Africa," said Heinrich. "They live in India. There are lions and leopards, but they won't hurt you except in self-defense, and we have guns."

"You ought to talk to our brother-in-law, Harold. He's in finance," said Kem.

"I'd like to go," said Rex. "I read Stanley's description of East Africa. It sounds exciting."

"Nairobi is a regular town now," said Heinrich. "There's a hotel where Stanley used to stay, called the Norfolk. Lord Delamere shot lions from the roof once. The old-timers still talk about it around the bar."

Doris felt as if something had changed in her life. There was an hour ago when things were as they always had been, and there was now. Africa. She looked at Heinrich, who was talking seriously to Rex. He was different from the other men she knew, different even from her older brother, Vern. She thought she must be in love with him. She knew it could happen like this—suddenly, without any warning. But now that it had happened, what did it mean? She felt she had been handed some unknown object without any instructions. And suppose he didn't want her? She thought of Grace and then Billy.

"Dor," Kem was waving at her. "Wake up! We're going to show Heinrich the village." He meant the pub.

As they were leaving, Mother showed up and was introduced. She looked hard at Heinrich. "Come for dinner and meet Mr. Pynegar," she said. "He would like to hear about your adventures."

"Thank you," he said. "it will be a pleasure." He took Doris's hand. I like you, his eyes said.

Doris could have hugged her mother, but she didn't. Displays of affection were not encouraged. "What do you think of him?" she asked when the men had gone.

"I'm not sure," said her mother. "He's older and looks experienced. That pretty face could hide a lot of things. We'll see what Da thinks."

"Of course he's different. He lives in Africa." Doris heard the sharp tone in her voice and knew her mother wouldn't like it.

"Don't be rude to me, miss," Mother said, "You read too many books for your own good. Mr. Heyman looks the sort who could ruin a woman's life."

That evening they all gathered around the dining room table. It was Sunday, and Daddy sharpened the knife to carve the joint. Jesse and Harold were there, and Heinrich showed up with a bottle of wine for Daddy and a huge box of chocolates. He had changed into what looked like new clothes—fashionably cut and made of the finest worsted cloth. Doris saw her mother examining him as he talked to Harold about investments. Doris sat on his right side next to Kem.

"What do you think of our new friend?" Kem asked as they watched the plates of lamb and roast potatoes go around. Kem was her favorite brother—even closer than her twin, Rex. He was less boyish in some ways than his brothers, not the first to jump up for a game of football but happy to sit and talk with Dor and Mother. He never said, Come off it, Dor—why not have Billy Bennett?—the way Reg might do. Kem knew Billy was wrong for her, as nice as he was. Too nice, said Kem, you'd make him miserable.

"He's good looking," said Doris in a low voice as she handed Kem the bowl of Brussels sprouts. "When is he going back to Africa?"

Kem shrugged, "When he raises some money."

"Mother thinks there is something odd about him."

"You grow up in Africa, and there might be something odd about you. He's just a little different. Sees the world from another angle, you might say."

Before she could ask more, Heinrich turned to her with a smile, as if he knew he was being discussed. She noticed how white his teeth were and that his beard had a lot of red in it. She thought of how the sun came through the stained glass window in the chapel at school. One of the squares had been the color of his beard. He must have seen her face change because, when she looked at his eyes, they knew something even she was only just aware of. In that moment they stopped being strangers.

Doris put down her knife and fork. "Tell me about Africa. What is it like?"

"For a woman?" asked Heinrich, as if he knew the real reason for her question. "If you have any adventure in you, you would love it. My mother says she will never leave. In fact, she likes it more than my father, who misses the European countryside." He helped himself to some more meat.

"Adventure," said Doris. She felt something flutter up into her throat. "I like going to Paris," she said.

He smiled. "It's not like Paris. It's much larger and more beautiful. When you ride out across the plains, you can see the sky from one end to the other. There are all kinds of flowers and animals to look at, and not many people."

"Wouldn't it be lonely?" she asked, thinking of her family.

"Not if you are with someone you love."

The table was being cleared and the deserts brought in. There was a rhubarb fool and an apple tart and a rice pudding. No matter what else there was, Daddy always finished with rice pudding. He said it filled up the cracks. Afterwards they went into the lounge for coffee, and Daddy beckoned to Heinrich. Doris helped her mother put away the food and listened to her instruct the cook. She noticed that Harold had gone over to talk to her father and Heinrich. Her father was smoking a cigar and saying something to Harold. Heinrich stood on one side.

"Do you think Daddy likes him?" Doris asked her mother. She knew she should keep quiet but she couldn't help it.

"Careful, or you'll make a fool of yourself." Her mother sounded angry, but Doris knew she was only worried. She thought Doris was too interested in men for her own good. A girl like that could wind up with a baby and no husband. Why wouldn't her father like him? thought Doris. He liked most of her brother's friends. Heinrich had no obvious faults. Yet there was something too vigilant in her mother's attitude. Nothing had happened, yet Doris felt events were moving beyond her control.

After that day, she saw a lot of Heinrich. They went walking into the village for tea, and sometimes she met him in London after she did her shopping. He took her to lunch and they spent some hours at Kew Gardens or visiting an exhibition. For the next six months, he became a regular visitor at Tamar.

When he was not with her, Heinrich was trying to raise money for his company. Harold put him in touch with some influential men with access to the kind of funds Heinrich needed. He consulted Henry Pynegar and discussed the nature of his idea with Reg and Kem. Reg thought he might return to Kenya with him. Within six months, Heinrich became a member of the family. No one said anything, but there was acceptance of Doris and Heinrich as a couple. There was no doubt they were in love. She was 19 and he was 10 years older. They were not children. Doris, who had always thought herself different from her sisters and her friends in school, felt that at last her life was on the right path. Unlike many young women of her class and age, she wanted something more than the boy next door and a comfortable life. She was discovering that she wanted adventure. The prospect of leaving home for Kenya excited rather than frightened her. She pored over the maps Heinrich brought.

He told her everything he could of life in the highlands above the Rift Valley. It was a hard life, he told her, in spite of the servants and the climate. The weather was unpredictable, as were the people. For this reason, he wanted to start a business in traveling and game hunting rather than farming the land. These were less subject to the weather and would help the economy by employing local labor.

And what about the Germans? Kem finally asked the question. Heinrich replied there were many Germans in East Africa. They had farms in Tanganyika, and others came to Kenya to hunt. But now no one wanted to invest in a business in Africa, no matter what a good idea it was. After six months, Heinrich was no further along than he had been when he came, except that he knew a lot of people and he was in love. His money was running out, and his father wired him twice to return home to help with the farm.

Doris knew her father would not let her go, even before anyone asked. Her mother was torn between sympathy for her daughter and anger at what she saw as Heinrich's irresponsible behavior.

"He should be thrashed," she fumed, "insinuating himself into the family and all but proposing to a young girl before he has anything to offer."

"He didn't know there was going to be a war," said Kem, defending his friend.

Heinrich and Doris knew it was over. They saw each other once or twice more. Doris was prepared to go with him, but he had no money left—his father had to wire him enough for his own passage. She had no resources of her own and no one would have backed what would have been seen as a suicidal move. Playing her last card—the affection her father felt for her—she begged him to let her go. She succeeded only in feeling the force of Victorian patriarchy. He was furious, and for months would have nothing to do with her.

Heinrich's idea for a safari business in East Africa came of age later, between the two world wars. Perhaps Heinrich became part of it if he was not killed in the war. They never heard of him again.

World War I came to England like the Black Death of the Middle Ages. It lasted four years and took almost an entire generation of young men. Like all other patriotic Englishmen, the Pynegar brothers enlisted to fight the Huns, to teach the Kaiser a lesson. Two died: Kem, the funniest, and Sylv, the youngest. Vern, the oldest, died 10 years after the armistice, perhaps of gas or war wounds. Sylv, who could not have been more than 15 or 16 in the early days of the war, lied about his age after some boys sent him a white feather, implying cowardice. This goaded him into enlisting. He died in the first days of trench warfare. Kemys died of the flu after armistice was declared.

Doris rolled bandages for the hospital and tried to help with surgery, but always ended by vomiting into some of the clean linen and having to be taken out. Gladys was better at it and helped Jesse run one of the local auxiliaries that provided bandages and collected gloves and socks for the men at the front.

When Rex returned home after the war, he said he despised Europe and what had happened to England. Two of his brothers were dead and his family in shock. There was no work. He was going to Australia to start a new life in a new economy. He liked the idea of sheep farming and empty spaces. No one argued with him. He wrote home for a time after he found work in Queensland, and was saving to buy his own land. He never returned to England.

Bill Bennett came to visit Tamar during his furloughs. Father was always glad to see him. With the older boys gone, he helped to fill some of the emptiness and was a steady, reassuring presence. He had not proposed to Doris for years and had never really been taken seriously when he did, but now Father, worried about the future of his business, was his champion. Gladys, three years younger than Doris, was already engaged.

One day, her father called Doris in to his study. It was no time for family estrangements, he told her; the country was in terrible shape and their family—his eyes wandered off to the window and he paused—was all they had left. He cleared his throat.

Doris could hardly bear to see her father like this. She knew Mother would survive and one day regain her sense of humor, but she was not sure about Daddy. Before Heinrich, she had loved him more than anyone, even more than Kem. The months after Heinrich left had been more terrible because he would not talk to her. Now he needed her again to help him bear the loss of his sons. She looked down at her hands. They were thin, and the knuckles, enlarged by repeated chilblains, looked uglier than ever. Mother worried about her hands and insisted on washing the dishes so she and Gladys could keep theirs looking nice, being young and unmarried. Now Doris covered one hand with the other in a gesture she kept all her life.

Father's hair and beard had gone quite gray, and he had become thinner. Still a large man, he now stooped forward as if he could no longer stand straight without his paunch. Mother had not changed except to sit more erect and tighten her mouth to what was now a permanent line.

"I want you to marry Bill Bennett," Father was saying.

"I don't love him, Daddy," said Doris. She could hardly get out the words.

"You must like him—there is nothing about him not to like. He is a good, kind man who will be a steady husband."

Doris felt nothing. "I don't think we can be happy," she said. But in the end, she agreed. She could not imagine any kind of happiness anyway.

CHAPTER 13

Bill and Doris

On his next leave, in December 1918, Bill and Doris were married in Blechingley, Surrey, at the parish church. They left the church under the raised swords of the Queen's Royal West Surrey Regiment. It was a month after the armistice, and Bill was posted to a remote district in India where the Army did not encourage wives to accompany their husbands. So Doris stayed behind once again, even though, in spite of threats of danger and discomfort, she wanted to go. Before that, it was clear she had been right about the marriage. She was not happy.

Kemys Deverell, my brother, named after Doris's favorite brother and his father's great grandmother, was born in St. Ives, Cornwall, on February 9, 1919, while Bill was in India. Doris had been sent to Cornwall because she had once again come down with pleurisy, which was complicated by her pregnancy. In Cornwall, she was given Guinness stout once a day. "A baby in every bottle," went the ad. Whether it was the stout or the sun and the sea, she recovered and produced a 10-pound son. She would have stayed in St. Ives, except that her husband returned, retired from the Army, and took a job as director of the Forgrove Machinery Works in Leeds, Yorkshire.

Doris and Bill and Kem lived in a row house opposite the park in Harrogate, a pretty town known for its baths and mineral waters. Doris must have preferred Harrogate over Leeds as a place to live, and Bill would have agreed. His commute to the Works in Leeds was not far. Doris took Kem to the park, did her shopping, read novels by Eleanor Glyn, the *Tatler,* and perhaps some Byron or Keats, books given to her before her marriage. The char came once a week to clean.

But it was hard to escape the coal mines that covered everything with a black oily film. Slag heaps were common, as were men with black faces coming home from work. You could smell the coal in the air; it blackened curtains and men's lungs.

Doris hated the long cold winters, the smell of coal, and the thick Yorkshire dialect. Bill was a good provider and a kind and thoughtful husband. He liked to come home from work and putter in the garden. Like many men of his generation, he had little use for bathing, especially in the winter. This did not make him attractive to his wife, who was sensual and fastidious, with a lifelong keen sense of smell.

Whether this was the reason or whether she was angry at him for not being someone else, Doris stopped sleeping with him.

"You are cruel," he said.

She shrugged. "I can't help it."

It must have been in these early days of marriage that she learned her way around the kitchen with the help of *Mrs. Beaton's Book of Household Management,* the definitive cookbook of the time. This book accompanied us everywhere and was consulted later in Portugal when we had a cook and much later in the United States when we didn't. Mrs. Beaton determined the form of the food we ate.

This cookbook, first written before the turn of the century, was designed to instruct young woman on housewifery. It assumed the existence of maids, but it also assumed diligence in attention to details of cleanliness and food preparation. If there were maids, they were to be strictly instructed in these matters. The recipes were a happy blend of English and French. The steamed or baked pudding and pie (sweet or savory) and the famous joint of beef or mutton was British soul food. French cooking influenced the preparation of vegetables—*petits pois, haricots verts,* and *aubergines*—in ways that preserved their natural flavor rather than boiling them to death as the English did.

As a child, my favorite desert was steamed puddings and treacle tarts. The puddings, steamed in boiling water in a basin covered with wax paper and a cloth and tied with a piece of string were made with beef suet, white flour, eggs, butter, and milk poured over some Lyle's Golden Syrup in the bottom of the basin. When done, the whole thing was turned out onto a plate, the hot syrup flowing over the pudding, smelling of butter and sugar. Treacle tarts were made with pastry dough—my mother had light hand—and filled with the same Lyle's Syrup, then covered with bread crumbs.

Later, when we were poor, my mother would remember earlier times, and she would exclaim that a modest piece of meat or chicken would feed a family of four for a week. As teenagers, when my sister and I rejected the fried bread she was so fond of, she reminded us that families had raised strapping sons on a diet of bread and dripping. We didn't care; we wanted to improve our figures and eating bread soaked in bacon fat was not going to do it.

Doris combined the ruggedness of the English character—tough as old boots, my brother was to say of her in her old age—and the sensuality of the French. This didn't play well in England where "putting on airs" or "playing to the gallery" were disapproved of by her family.

Doris was naturally thrifty and able to save something from her weekly housekeeping allowance to put aside for holidays. Travel became her greatest pleasure.

She read about France and Switzerland and pored over maps. She read about Alpine flowers and ski runs and Mont Blanc and Lausanne and the Castle of Chillon near Montreux on Lake Geneva. She read about Paris and the artists who lived around Montparnasse and the Left Bank. She started remembering Mademoiselle's lessons. But Bill was kept busy at the Works and now could take little time off.

When Doris and Bill were first married, before he left the Army, they took holidays during his home leave in France and Switzerland. He would have a pocket full of money when they met in Paris to go "on the razzle" to small hotels and French music halls where the wine was cheap.

Once, she met him in Vevey and, in honor of the occasion, bought a bottle of Italian Chianti. In those days, the bottles were often not professionally corked but simply bottled where the grapes were harvested and sold locally in small quantities. Doris carried her bottle back to the small hotel room and decided to taste the wine. She carefully poured a small amount into a glass and tossed it down. Just as rapidly, she spat it out. The bottle had been topped with olive oil to prevent air from entering and spoiling the wine, which was corked by hand. When Bill arrived, she would have met his train at the little station. They went back to the hotel and she poured him a glass then told him her experience with the wine. He would have said "poor old Dor," because that was the way as children they had expressed sympathy for an honorable hurt.

Even though she left him and lived the last half of her life outside her country, their speech remained the same, having come from the same roots. When I visited my father after being separated for five years during the war, I recognized the language as soon as he spoke. Even the inflections and expressions were the same as hers. They shared a dialect spoken by no one else I ever knew. I would have heard it at Tamar in Beckenham, sitting at the table next to her brothers or my grandparents.

When Kem was six, like all middle class boys and their fathers before them, he was sent to boarding school. Doris took him on school holidays to the Continent. They crossed the channel to Calais, then took a train to Switzerland and stayed in inexpensive *pensiones* or small hotels near Vevey or St. Moritz, where they pulled the small sleds she called *luges* up the slopes and whizzed down, Doris in front and Kem clinging to her waist. Madame, the *propriétaire*, fed the guests the same food she gave the family: the thick *potage* that began every dinner, *poulet à l'ancienne* or meat, cheese and fruit, wine. They were very happy there, and Kem learned to love France and prefer the refinements of French food and wine to the homelier cooking of England.

"*Je suis plein,*" Kem said after a full meal.

Madame laughed. "*Non, mon enfant, tu dois dire 'j'ai bien mangé.' Tu n'es pas enceinte!*"

Doris gave her son the affection she couldn't give her husband, and these holidays allowed her to leave northern England with its black air and cold damp weather. In the Alps, she got up every morning to clear air, sun, and white snow. Her breakfast was freshly baked bread, coffee with milk, homemade preserves. In the evening the guests sat around the lounge, and Doris enjoyed being a woman alone with a pretty child. She had lost some of her earlier shyness and liked the attention she got from the other guests—especially the men, who did not seem to find her posturing or artificial, as she was accused of being at home. Italian and French men were interested in her clothes—something Englishmen did not notice. Did she go back to their rooms with them in the evening after her son was safely asleep? Perhaps—but she had no children in the 13 years between my brother's birth and my own.

During this period, she gradually became "Sylvia," rather than "Dor," and felt more at home on the Continent than in England.

These holidays were important times in her life when she learned to love places instead of people, to prefer, as so many English have, to live outside their small demanding island with its illustrious past and yet remain, in exile, completely English.

She undoubtedly looked younger than she was, as she did throughout her life due to excellent posture, heavy dark brown hair, clear white skin, and a beautiful figure. She knew she was no beauty, but she was attractive to men and all her life preferred their company. She was sensual, and sentimental rather than warm, with a sense of humor and flexibility of temperament that helped her survive. She was capable of anger and later bitterness but in spite of "the little blue devils" that sometimes visited, she was never, as she said, a "miserable person." A laugh and a drink, and she was back in business.

She alienated her family when she visited her parents and married sisters by putting on "Frenchified" airs. "*Ooo-la-la!*" she exclaimed when she dropped her handkerchief. Her nieces collapsed in giggles at Auntie Dor, her sisters would roll their eyes, and Granny would tighten her mouth. After I was born, Granny refused to call me by my French name, Simone Sylvia, but dubbed me "Sally." Doris wouldn't argue with her mother, but later she told her sisters she wanted to be called "Sylvia" instead of "Doris." Up went the eyebrows. But she was adamant, for all the good it did her. They never called her anything but "Dor." However, for the rest of her life, she was "Sylvia" to herself and everyone else who knew her, including her children.

CHAPTER 14

Sylvia and Jack

It was at this time in Portugal that my Mother told me how she had come to know Jack. I knew, of course, that he was not my father but I had never heard how they met. Was I old enough to be told? No one ever asks if children are old enough. We were alone, and my mother needed someone to talk to.

Bill had asked Doris if he might bring a visitor home for dinner—an American engineer brought over to discuss new mining techniques. Bill had visited Chicago and known some Yanks in the Army. "Nice blokes," he said. Doris had never known any Americans and was curious. They were generally thought of in England as "savages" or cowboys. So when Jack Pratt arrived, wearing a Savile Row suit with a box of chocolates from Fortnum & Mason, Doris was first surprised, then delighted. He was tall and dark with a quick mind and a warm easy manner. The chemistry between them was immediate.

Doris wore a white chiffon dress that clung to her body, and had pulled her dark brown hair back in waves coiled at the back of her neck in a chignon. Bill introduced her as "Doris," but she confided to Jack later that she preferred "Sylvia."

"'Who is Sylvia?'" he quoted with a smile. "'What is she, that all the swains commend her?'"

"I didn't know Americans knew English poetry."

"We are not complete ignoramuses, despite what you might have heard."

By the time Bill returned with the drinks, Doris felt she had known
Jack always. That is the way with love. He smelled good, was beautifully dressed, and lived in Spain, not America. She knew he wanted
her; he hardly bothered to hide it. Before that first evening was over,
they had kissed.

After he left, Doris and Bill were doing the dishes. "Interesting
chap," said Bill. "What did you think of him?"

Doris asked, "How long is he going to be here?"

"Dunno. We've finished with him, but he's going around to some
other firms. Knows a lot about mines. Got interested when he was a
child in the mountains of Kentucky and Tennessee." Bill stopped wip-
ing his plate and stared into space. "Grew up among hillbillies, he told
me. Now he wears Savile Row suits." Bill grinned, "I had to ask him
what a hillbilly was."

"What is it?" asked Doris. For reasons she could not identify, the
conversation was making her uneasy. She wanted this man to be what
she wanted him to be—not some stranger with a bizarre background.

"Someone who lives in the mountains, makes whiskey and can't
read or write."

"But he isn't like that," said Doris.

"He stole a pair of shoes so he could go to school." Bill hung up
his towel. "I'll put the kettle on." They always had tea before going to
bed.

Doris rinsed out the pot and put two cups and saucers on a tray.
She was thinking of his kiss. She did not feel any guilt or fear for the
future. Sexual arousal had disarmed any warning signals. Did Bill know
what was coming? Did he care? If he knew, his reticence would not
have allowed him to intervene. He had always loved her the way you
love someone you cannot have. She made him miserable, but he never
complained. When she told him she was in love with Jack, he begged
for another chance—that they go on a second honeymoon and try
again.

I suppose she felt she could not refuse, although she knew it was wouldn't work, didn't want it to work. They went to Cornwall for a month and walked along the sea wall in St. Ives, where she been sent with pleurisy and where Kem was born. Once more, they slept together in the same bed. Bill was his gentlest self, but she felt nothing. When they returned home, Doris was pregnant.

When Jack came to England, six months later, she agreed to see him to say goodbye.

"You cannot send me away," Jack said. "These last six months have been unbearable."

"Look at me," she said. She was very large. Kem had weighed 10 pounds and this one would be near that weight, the doctor had said.

Jack knelt in front of her and buried his face in her skirt. "You look beautiful. I'll never let you go."

He was true to his word. He remained as close as possible, appearing for a few days at a time, writing, sending flowers. Somehow, Bill did not know of Jack's presence, although Doris made no effort to hide anything. She put his flowers in the drawing room, left his letters lying about. Once Jack forgot his hat and it hung on the coat rack in the hall for a week until he returned. Bill saw nothing. He admired the flowers without asking where they came from, never read a letter not addressed to him, ignored the hat. He knew Doris was not happy, but he believed the baby would change everything.

Did my mother try to make the marriage work after I was born? My brother, 13 at the time, was away at school. Later she would tell me that "it was no good." I took that to mean that a new baby changed nothing compared to her attraction to Jack Pratt—whom Granny referred to as a "fancy man."

I was born at home in Harrogate in the little semi-detached house across from the park.

Within two years, Doris had asked Bill for a divorce, and this time he gave in. He arranged everything, and when the divorce was final she left with me and Nanny and traveled to London, where she and Jack were married. He meanwhile had terminated his marriage to the previously unheard-of Elsie.

She told me Bill had sent flowers when she and Jack were married. I thought she would have preferred them to have fought over her. After this, my mother left England, not to return as a resident until 1946. She left her son, Kem, behind in boarding school and in the care of his father.

CHAPTER 15

Fraulein

One day the doorbell rang again. We had had no visitors since the two maids. I looked over the side of the balcony and saw a young woman with short, curly brown hair, dressed neatly in a suit. She looked familiar. The small boy standing next to her was younger than my sister. When the gate buzzed, they started up the steps to the house. Excited at the prospect of a visitor, I ran downstairs. I found my mother and the woman shaking hands in the hall.

"You remember Fraulein?" My mother's voice was tense.

Fraulein, my German nurse! The woman turned to face me, smiling. She seemed to be trying to decide whether to give me a hug. I could not move. She used to help me dress and braid my hair. But since then, I had seen newsreels of bombs blowing up England, trains full of starving people, and at the end, hideous pictures of concentration camps. The woman put out her hand and said something in German. I looked at my mother.

"I'm afraid she's forgotten the German you taught her," my mother said coldly.

Fraulein put her arm around the boy next to her. "My son, Stefan," she said in English with a heavy accent. The child clicked his heels together and flung up his arm in a Nazi salute. I felt my mouth open and saw my mother's lips tighten. Fraulein gently pushed his arm down. She lifted her shoulders. "He cannot remember."

"I will not have it in this house!" My mother's voice rose at the end like Winston Churchill's.

Stefan stared impassively at her. Raised voices were nothing to him. Fraulein flushed and said something sharply to him in German. The boy's face twisted. He hissed at his mother. She hit him hard on the side of his head. He staggered back, then opened his mouth and howled. I felt the hair on my arms stand up. I had never heard a sound like that. It was not an animal's sound or a child's.

Fortunately, at that moment, his nose started to bleed. Both women were united by the sight of blood. My mother went to the kitchen for some cold water, and Fraulein made him lie down. When the bleeding stopped, he was wiped off and the drops of blood cleaned off the floor.

"We could all use a cup of tea," said Sylvia. She sounded very cheerful, very British.

I put on the kettle and opened a new tin of Favorita chocolate-covered biscuits. Sylvia carried the tray upstairs to the small table by the window. Fraulein and Stefan followed. Janine was playing when we all came in, and Fraulein took her in her arms. Janine looked surprised but didn't resist.

"You are not a baby anymore," Fraulein said and released her. I could not tell if Janine remembered her nurse; she had been only three when we left. No one said anything while the tea was poured and the biscuits handed around. Fraulein, reassured by Sylvia's cheerful tone, was examining her surroundings.

"Everything is just the same," she said in her halting English. "Even the little window between the rooms." She pointed this out to her son, talking to him in German. He ignored her.

I glanced at the little window. I knew it was there so our nurse could look in on us without having to disturb us by opening the door. I had never seen one anywhere else. I hadn't liked being spied on, I had told my mother one day, although I couldn't remember feeling anything about the window when I was little.

Spied on? Sylvia lifted her plucked brows. I didn't like it when my mother did that; it looked fake and old-fashioned.

"Why don't you have any eyebrows?" I once demanded.

"When I was young, it was fashionable to pluck them out, and they never grew back."

I couldn't imagine doing such a thing.

Fraulein was telling us about Germany. She had a husband, she said, but he was killed and left nothing to provide for her and the boy. Now there was no work. Could she stay here? She would do any-thing—clean the house, cook, give us lessons. She wanted only food for herself and her son.

I stared at the blond child. There was a red welt in front of his left ear and there were bloodstains on his jacket. I had never seen anyone hit a child like that before. I offered him the chocolate biscuits. He glanced quickly at me, then turned away. I didn't want him to live with us.

"We might not stay," said Sylvia. "I might sell the house and return to England."

Fraulein looked down at her hands. "We used to be valuable," she said. "Now we are garbage." She raised her eyes. "It happened so fast."

I caught myself holding my breath and stopped.

"England! I don't want to go there." I stood up, feeling my breath racing inside my chest. "I want to go back to America."

"That's enough. Now you're being rude."

I rushed out the door into the dressing room and curled up in the old chair. In a little while I heard the front door close. When I looked over the balcony, Fraulein and the boy were walking down the road toward the sea, just as the two maids had done. A lot of people had left. I wished some replacements would show up. Parts of our old life kept reappearing, then disappearing again. It was like being on a boat. You drifted near to shore and, just when you thought the tide was going to carry you in, the current took you back out to sea, and all you could do was watch the beach get further and further away.

When Mummy came in and stroked my hair, I asked her if we had to go to England.

"We can't stay here, dearest. We have family in England." She pulled me up and sat down, then pulled me back down on her lap. "We belong there now."

I let myself lean into my mother's neck even though I did not usually tolerate being hugged or kissed. I breathed in her distinctive smell underneath the warmth and the perfume. This was how animals found their mothers in the herd; your own smelled like no one else.

"Why can't we go back to America?"

"We don't have anywhere to go."

"We could go back to Asheville. Connie's there, and Mrs. Bull."

"We were only there for the war," said Sylvia. "We don't really belong; it's Jack's country." She sounded tired and sad.

"We've never been to England—not to live."

"I grew up there, remember?" Sylvia smiled. "But I liked Europe better—or I did. Now everything is different."

"I don't want to go."

"It's your country," said Sylvia. She leaned down to kiss me.

I turned my head. The hairs that now grew around my mother's mouth tickled, and I didn't like the feeling.

CHAPTER 16
Goodbye, Portugal

I didn't think I had a country. When we went into Lisbon to see the lawyer, there were lots of people and cars, like in America, but it still seemed very different from American cities. Black-shawled women hawked oranges and fish and cakes. Knife grinders were common and boys or old men herded turkeys through the streets. If anything—anything—out of the ordinary happened, a crowd immediately gathered. Once, Sylvia slipped on a wet pavement and fell, tearing her stockings and losing a heel from her shoe. While I helped her up, ten people stopped to watch. They stared silently while I tried to put the heel back on the shoe. A man came over, took it from me and motioned us to sit on a curb. He left with the shoe.

"Do you think he'll come back?" I asked.

"I hope so," said Sylvia. "What would he want with one old shoe?" She laughed, but looked worried. Half an hour passed. Finally, the man reappeared. He handed Sylvia the shoe, its heel restored. *Obrigado, muy obrigado*, said Sylvia, clutching her shoe. She opened her purse for money but he waved it off and left. Our little crowd melted away. "Simple people," said Sylvia. "It warms the heart." She looked happier than she had for weeks, and I felt the tightness loosen inside my chest.

We went to a chocolate shop to celebrate. Inside, you were cocooned in the smell of cocoa. I ordered hot chocolate, closed my eyes, and sucked it in. Sucking food was another bad habit my mother hated.

Meanwhile, Sylvia ordered hot tea. "I used to get my Jordon almonds here," she said, "and your Easter eggs. Do you remember the chocolate eggs filled with sugar babies?"

At the beginning of spring term, Janine and I were enrolled in an English school in Carcavellos, a small town on the coast between Estoril and Lisbon. All the students wore green skirts or trousers, blazers, and a striped tie. Boys wore caps, girls brimmed hats. We took the train every morning from Estoril to Carcavellos, and then back at the end of the school day. I remember buying chocolate bars from a machine in the station (I was a fool for chocolate in those days) and memorizing poems by John Masefield—"Cargoes" and "West Wind"—that I can recite to this day. I was there too short a time to make friends, or if I did, that memory has disappeared. School was one short episode in the brief but turbulent period we spend in Portugal.

When the winter was at its coldest and the only warm place was bed, Sylvia woke one morning with a headache and sore throat. She wrapped a scarf around her neck and drank a lot of hot tea. The next day she felt worse. Her temperature was over 100 degrees. It rose to 102 by evening. She took aspirin and slept. I made her tea and brought cold cloths for her head. The next day she started coughing. Then she became delirious and muttered names I did not recognize. Sometimes she laughed and seemed to be having a conversation, but the words were never clear. On the fourth day, I got frightened. I had no idea what to do. We had not called a doctor since I had chicken pox in Savannah. I must have helped Sylvia to the bathroom and brought her water, but those details have left me.

One evening, my mother lifted up her head and looked straight at me. "Take care of Janine." Then she lay back down and closed her eyes.

I fixed some scrambled eggs for Janine and a pot of tea for Sylvia when she woke up. Then I put Janine to bed. She went right to sleep as if she knew better than to stay awake. I opened the front door and stood outside. The air was wet and cold. There were no lights anywhere and no stars, only a faint glow in the sky above Estoril. In America there were streetlights even in the small towns. Here they stopped at the park before the road started to wind up the hill. I saw a dark shape by the gate. Two yellow eyes looked up. One of the cats. Their eyes reflected the light even when there wasn't any. The shape slipped away. I turned and went back into the house and locked the door. Inside, the air smelled stale, of cold plaster and cooking oil. Upstairs, Sylvia coughed.

The bedroom was warmer because of the electric fire, but didn't smell any better than the hall. I put down the tray and went to look at my mother. I felt her head. It was hot. Her breathing had gotten noisy because her mouth was now open. I lifted her head off the pillow and tried to plump it up, but the pillow was wet. I took the pillow off my bed and stuck it under my mother's head, raising her up. She opened her eyes.

"Mama?"

She took a sharp breath and coughed. Some yellow stuff came out of her mouth. Her eyes lost their focus and then closed.

I wiped my mother's mouth. I was determined to be cheerful. Sylvia had no patience with being miserable, and this was no time to make her angry. And I had to take care of Janine. I ate my scrambled eggs and poured a cup of tea. Sylvia's mouth was open again and she was breathing heavily. I touched her cheek. It was very soft. She always had the softest skin. I don't want you to die, I thought; I want you to be happy.

Sylvia gave a terrible cough and groaned. "I'm not mad at you anymore," I said. "I love you." I had not told her that since we left America.

I went into the cold hall, through my mother's old bedroom and into the dressing room. There must have been a hundred books on the shelves—some of them stacked on the floor. I had read them all, many more than once. Starting at the top shelf, I scanned every title one at a time, looking for help. Some of the novels had doctors in them. I took down one or two and read a little. There was description, but no practical information. I was afraid to go back into the bedroom. Some things might not be in books. Things you needed to know. This thought surprised and disappointed me. If life outside books was so unpredictable and books did not tell you either, how could you ever know what to do? What could you believe? I heard a sound from the other room and rushed toward it. Sylvia had fallen sideways over the side of the bed. Her breathing was faster and more ragged. I took my mother's hand. I felt a terrible loneliness and started to cry.

Sometime during the night I fell asleep. When I woke, a faint light was coming in the window. I heard the cocks crowing at a nearby farm. A dog barked. I had let go of my mother's hand and slid down onto the floor, leaning against the side of the bed. I could no longer hear her breathing. She was lying on her back quite still. Her eyes were closed. How do you know when someone's dead? I touched my mother's hand. It was cool. Then I remembered reading about the mirror. It was difficult to hold her hand mirror under her nostrils because it had a silver back. Then I saw two little spots of mist form on the very edge. "Mama!" I shouted.

Sylvia's eyes opened. She blinked. "Hello darling," she said. "What time is it?" Her voice was very faint.

I held my breath, then remembered to let it out. "Early," I said. "But it's morning."

CHAPTER 17

1946: England

Sylvia's illness was the final proof she needed to convince her that there could be no life for us any longer in Portugal. It was still a country where a single woman was at a disadvantage, and being a foreigner with no family or friends and two young children to raise was too difficult. She decided we would return to England—our country, after all.

I did not want to go to England. I said I wanted to return to America. My mother tightened her lips and told me not to be rude. She notified the lawyer, and the house was put on the market. It must have sold right away because we were soon on our way to England.

It was early summer when we arrived. Aunt Jesse, Sylvia's oldest sister, and Uncle Harold met us at the airport and drove us to their home, Coombe Down House, in the village of Ditchling in Sussex. London was in shambles with gaping holes everywhere and piles of rubble. The countryside, however, showed little sign of war damage. Birds sang from the hedgerows; all nature was green and gold. Coombe Down House was a country dream with its rose garden, green lawns, and rabbits diving into the hedgerows as we passed.

Uncle Harold had made his fortune in London real estate and he and my aunt lived a modified prewar life. They had servants and still dressed for dinner. The gardener grew their vegetables and they kept chickens and ducks beyond the hedge: "the 'edge—the 'edge," said the cook crossly, when I was sent to find eggs for breakfast.

One of their two sons, Ashleigh, was educated at Oxford where he had been a star athlete at the 1932 Olympic Games in Munich when the British team refused to salute Hitler. I remember Ashleigh and Pam, his wife, as an elegant and kind couple living in beautiful surroundings on the edge of the New Forest in a retirement village where the wild ponies visited the garden to eat the flowers.

John, Aunt Jesse's youngest son, was devious and unkind but adored by his mother. He had been injured in a motorcycle accident, and this was the excuse given for his bad behavior and general failures.

Uncle Harold lived up to his reputation as a diamond in the rough when, one night at dinner, he heaved a tomato at my sister, then ten years old. Nothing was said. Father was just being father.

A diamond he was in all but manners. He supported my grandfather and grandmother in their old age. He was generous to his wife and her family and tolerated his feckless younger son.

As a young adolescent, I was always on the lookout for information on sex. One day in the car, passing a field full of cows and one bull, I noticed the bull mounting a heifer. What is he doing, I asked? Was it like the cats but larger? Just playing, muttered Uncle Harold. He bought his wife a fancy new car, and I saw them exchange a passionate kiss in the driveway. I was not used to seeing adults in intimate moments.

While living at Coombe Down House, I discovered *Gone With the Wind* by Margaret Mitchell, and fell in love—not with the handsome hero, Rhett Butler, but with Scarlett. Like the younger heroines of books like *Green Mansions* and *Girl of the Limberlost,* she was independent and tough. Scarlett was a new woman, out of step with her time but beautiful and intelligent and determined to survive.

My mother kept pressing on me the 19th-century novels of Jane Austen and Charlotte Bronte, which I would later come to love. But then I had eyes only for Scarlett. Like her, I was angry at my helplessness. I did not want to be in England. I wanted to be in America again, and I wanted to be grown up.

Meanwhile, my mother found a semi-detached house in Hassocks the next village. Its long lawn bordered with lavender bushes ended in a small orchard of overgrown apple trees.

We had always had dogs, usually cocker spaniels, usually black. The last one was "Blackie" (a name we reused several times). During the war we forewent dogs in favor of the two wild squirrels that chewed up the sun porch. Now, "home" once more, we acquired two cocker spaniel puppies: one black, one golden, named Fifi and Kiki. These were names fashionable at the time because of two French actresses or models Sylvia must have admired. Sadly, both puppies got distemper, and, after foaming at the mouth and running in circles, they died. I was as fascinated by this as I had been by the squirrel expiring after its drop of medicinal brandy. Next came Tiger, a full-grown Golden Retriever who threw up whenever he got in a car.

Eventually, our furniture arrived from Portugal, and I was enrolled in Merton House School, a local private day school, owned and run by two women, Miss Merton and Miss Warburton, who divided up the teaching. This school required blue uniforms. The other girls teased me, calling me "celery" instead of "Sally."

"They wouldn't tease you if they didn't like you," said Miss Merton.

She might have been right, but it didn't matter. I had experienced the American school system, and nothing else would satisfy me. There had been boys and kissing games, and here there were ugly school uniforms and nothing but girls. We played field hockey, and I acquired my first tennis racquet: a small wooden one in a square press. I kept it for years, although I did not play again for a long time.

I did well enough in my studies, but not well enough to win any prizes except a class prize (I thought of it as the booby prize): a leather-bound book of Shakespeare's comedies, which I never read.

CHAPTER 18
Leyland House: Part One

In 1945, I saw my own father again for the first time since before the war. He met me in London, where we stayed in a hotel and went to the Chelsea Flower Show. During school holidays, I visited him in Yorkshire where he still lived in the same Georgian house in the village of Garforth on the Leeds-Selby road. In the '30s, it was only modestly traveled; today it is a major north-west artery. In 1945, he shared the house with his wife, Barbara, his daughter, Anne, and a small day school for preschool children. This was run by Miss Mary, a tiny white-haired woman with eyes like blue marbles. She giggled when she told me she used to pinch her brother in the bath to watch his mouth turn into an upside down "u."

At the time of my mother and father's divorce, the expectation must have been that my brother and I would travel back and forth during school holidays between England and Spain. But I don't remember Kem ever visiting us during the 1930s. I visited my father some summers, before the war made it impossible.

Although I visited infrequently and only for short periods, it was home to me. I was always given the same room in the front of the house, overlooking the garden. The windows were huge, with old wavy glass and no screens. There was no central heating and, only later, gas fires in the bedroom grates where there had originally been coal fires laid by servants. Downstairs was cozier, with comfortable furniture and long, red velvet drapes and fireplaces that burned the hard coal of the area.

I have always had special feelings about this house, its gardens, and the fields around. The people spoke my language and seemed familiar and normal in a way that the place and inhabitants of our life in Portugal did not.

Leyland House

My father hung a swing for me from a sturdy old apple tree next to the flower beds. Beyond them, he kept his beehives. The adjoining field was leased to a farmer who used it to pasture his dray horses. They kicked up their huge hoofs and frolicked with each other as if they were lambs. There was a summer house my father had transported from his childhood home in Surrey, which swiveled to allow you to avoid or catch the sun at any time of the day. Bill was a gardener and one of my earliest memories is the hot pungent smell of tomatoes in a greenhouse.

Before bed, Daddy read to me from *Alice in Wonderland*. The Cheshire cat appeared in several colored plates and disappeared a piece at a time until in the last picture the cat was invisible. This frightened me so much that my father cut out all the plates that showed the cat in the process of vanishing. As a book lover, this must have been difficult for him. But I had had my fill of things vanishing. I knew only too well that not only cats in books disappeared—it could happen to anyone.

I loved the large old music box that played a variety of old songs. The enameled insects struck the bells as the drum (it looked like a miniature piano roll) turned. I thought all these things were mine, or partly mine. I certainly felt a proprietary right. Later, after my father remarried and had a child, I learned what it felt like to have what I thought mine become someone else's.

There are some photos of these summer visits. Several are at the beach. In one, Kem is digging in the sand, rather like a dog, and I am watching. Above us, our father looks protectively into the middle distance. We are frozen in time: the two children and the father. There is only the beach and the sun and the little girl who is there on loan. We love each other but meet rarely because of distance, then the war. Gradually, we become strangers in whom there are echoes both disturbing and moving of this unrealized love.

Kem, Bill, and Sally c.1934–36

CHAPTER 19

Leyland House: Part Two

After the war, coal was still being mined throughout Yorkshire, especially near Leeds. The miners who waited by the road after a day's work had faces black from soot. It was a dirty place. Later I understood why my mother hated the black slag heaps and cold countryside. I saw it only in summer, when leaves hid some of the dirt and the sun warmed the dark ground.

"Go and talk to your father," my stepmother said, rousting me out of the corner where I was, as usual, deep in a book. I found him in the greenhouse. He smiled, always pleased to see me, although we never knew what to say to each other. So I sat and watched him, basking in the warm pungent smell of the tomatoes and his comfortable presence.

Periodically, he would put on his protective clothing, fire up the smoke machine, and remove the honeycombs from his hives. At those times, we were advised to stay indoors as the bees became agitated and apt to sting. I watched him dressed in baggy protective gear, squeezing an accordion-like machine that emitted clouds of smoke. Bees were everywhere and frantic. He calmly removed the trays of filled honeycombs and replaced them with empty ones. Then he closed the hive and carried the combs toward the kitchen door, bees and smoke trailing behind. He never seemed to get stung, but once I saw Barbara remove the stinger attached to a little ball of venom from my sister's arm. This was possible, she explained if you did not rub the sting first.

Besides the Victorian music boxes, my father collected glass paper-weights (many of them old and valuable) and books. He loved the Kate Greenaway children's books and owned first editions of Oliver Gold-smith and other 19th-century novelists as well as a complete set of works by the illustrator Aubrey Beardsley and an early copy of *Salome* by Oscar Wilde, also illustrated by Beardsley. He had a cellar full of wine from before the war, but he enjoyed collecting more than drink-ing, and some bottles were still there when I last saw him in 1964.

He gave me one of his paperweights and later Barbara gave me two of his books. When my father died, my brother, Kem, removed the Aubrey Beardsley collection and sold it. He and Barbara had never liked each other, and this must have ended their relationship. I once asked Kem why he disliked Barbara, and he replied that he had come to resent her when our father was courting her and she took so long to accept him, always putting him off until finally (Kem thought) no one better appeared, and she reluctantly accepted.

Barbara was furious when she discovered the Beardsley collection gone, even though neither she nor Anne was interested in them and, as far as I know, neither read any of the books. But they were, of course, valuable. Perhaps they drank the wine, but I doubt it. The music boxes, books, and paperweights were all sold after my father died. I was told they fetched a good price. But in 1945, when I met Barbara for the first time, I liked her. She treated me more like an adult than my mother did and made it clear she preferred me to my brother. I had reasons of my own to resent Kem, and found it easy to ally myself with Barbara against him. He was everything I was not. He was glamorous (a war hero), good-looking, and articulate (a writer). He was in many ways like my mother. They were both impractical, generous, and impulsive.

It was during my first visit to my father after the war, when I was 14, that Barbara introduced me to the occult. She told me that she had had supernatural experiences when she was young; apparitions came to her at night, accompanied at times by terrifying noises, and she could sense "presences" in houses. Her sister, who had slept in the same room, was never troubled. Barbara assured me that Leyland House was free of any troubling spirits. I believed her, but I was frightened by her stories. She was not a woman who dramatized her life; she was very private and even shy, probably anti-intellectual in the middle-class English way that considers any kind of "showing off" as bad form.

She was the very opposite of my mother, and it was probably for this as much as her affection for me that made me like her. I fantasized living with her and my father, but this would never have crossed my father's mind, and it was never proposed. Even if it had been, I could not have gone. I was tied to my mother in ways I did not then recognize.

Years later, when I was an adult, Barbara asked me if the stories had frightened me. I admitted they had, but by then I knew more and asked her if these "apparitions" ceased after she was married. She said yes. I thought to myself: Ah yes, sex. But I also knew the English were much more accepting of supernatural events than Americans. There are many supernatural legends, often located in famous bloodstained places such as the Tower of London. Some of the country houses now open to the public with entrance fees and tea rooms have resident ghosts that make irregular but recorded appearances. This is generally accepted without much fuss unless there is a noisy or destructive poltergeist or some other threat to civil order.

Years later, Kem took me to see the house where I was born. I was surprised that it was still there. I had not returned to Harrogate since I left at age two. When I visited my father, we made regular trips to York, a historic and interesting city, and to Leeds. Why had we never been to Harrogate? Why had I never asked to go? I can only think it was part of his life with my mother, which became a forbidden topic. Not that anyone ever forbade it; it was simply never mentioned.

Children learn to talk about what they hear. I heard nothing about my birthplace, an hour's drive away. Even more curious, I never thought about it until Kem took me there. Then I could think of nothing to ask. What worlds might have opened for my brother and me if we had been able to plunge into that forgotten abyss and discover our earliest selves? As it was, we paused at the end of the street facing the park—I can see it in my mind's eye—then drove away.

Since I never lived with my father or Kem, and only saw them a few times, I do not know much about their lives. All I know I learned during those brief periods of contact, most of them when I was a child. My half-sister, Anne, has lived her life near where she grew up and has been in touch with my father's family all her life. The history of the Bennett family comes from her although, sadly, there are few personal details.

CHAPTER 20

Bennett

William Deverell was born in 1887, making him four years older than my mother. He was probably brought up outside London in Sydenham (where the Pynegar family lived for a time). After leaving the army, Bill moved to Leeds, where some of the family had previously lived, to take over as a director, with his brother, of the Forgrove Machinery Works. He was educated in a public (private) school in Hurstpierpoint and then Dulwich Engineering College. After this, he joined the Queen's Royal West Surrey Regiment along with his father, brother, and two brothers-in-law. A photograph of these men show the four young officers standing behind the father who would tower above them if he were standing. Much taller and heavier than his sons, James William Bennett looks like a throwback to ancestors he refers to as "hefty chaps." (A letter to my father from my grandfather, James William Bennett, is reproduced in Appendix 1.)

Bill began courting Barbara Batley while Kem was at school. At holiday time, he was dragged along, "cap in hand" (his words), to visit and propose marriage once again. For years, Barbara refused, preferring to go along "as they were" for a number of years before she finally accepted.

Later, Kem referred to his father's "amiable heedlessness," which helped turn him into what he called a lone wolf. Kem inherited our mother's temperament: romantic and high-spirited, rather than practical and acquiescent.

Queen's Royal West Surrey Regiment. Left to right: Stanley Stedman, WIlliam Pryce, George Bennett, James WIlliam Bennett, William Deverell Bennett

My mother liked men and often had to live without her husband when he was in India and later when she took her young son to Europe for school vacations. There were rumors in the family that either Kem or myself was fathered by another man. But, as I came to resemble my father, the story of the second honeymoon went undisputed. Kem, on the other hand, looked much like one of my mother's brothers, but had little resemblance to my father's family.

All I know of my father was that, besides being an engineer, a gardener, a beekeeper, and a lover of books, he was also an admirer of Popeye the Sailor Man and, perhaps more strangely, gorillas. He had in his possession when he died some large glossy prints of a statue of a gorilla by the English sculptor David Wynne, which stands in Kensington Gardens in London. Bill was visiting the gorilla statue when a

Standing: unknown; seated: James Bennett and Anne Lister Bennett, 1931

photographer popped out from behind and offered to sell him some photographs, which he bought. David Wynne became the second husband of Kem's wife, Gillian Grant, who divorced my brother to marry him. When Kem lived in Joan Grant's house, David Wynn was a friend of the family, and Kem undoubtedly took our father to see the gorilla.

When I try to put together these few flags of my father's taste—his love of gardens and the natural world, glass paperweights, the erotic drawings of Beardsley, Kate Greenaway's Victorian children with their ribbons and hoops and skipping ropes, and then the macho symbolism of Popeye and the gorilla—it sounds like a well-rounded personality. But he was too subdued and repressed to have exhibited these characteristics, at least to his children. I wish I had known my father when I was growing up. But I take comfort in knowing these traits exist in some form in our gene pool.

I always believed my father loved me but was too remote both in distance and concern to show it. Even though we corresponded periodically, he never inquired about my education or anything else. I once asked him to pay for a secretarial course, which he did. He might have paid for college had I had the self-confidence to ask. In response to my desperate request, he paid my mother's passage to England when I got married, with the money that was to have been his wedding present to me. Kem's charge of "amiable heedlessness" seems about right.

After public school, Kem went to an engineering college—perhaps the same one my father attended. He hated school. When the war started, he signed up with the British Special Forces, the Commandoes, and was dropped behind enemy lines in Denmark to work with the Resistance. For this he was awarded a medal, the Danish Knight. He was wounded—almost fatally—in France. He told stories—always funny—of these experiences. He never told us what his medals were for and, as far as I know, never sent for them.

Like my mother's family, the Pynegars, he had an abundance of charm, high spirits, and humor. He told me once he thought we had always liked each other. For me this vastly understated my feelings for him, which for years were best described as adoration. He was, I thought, the most attractive man I could imagine, aside from movie stars and characters in books. This accounts for my pathological shyness on those rare occasions when we met.

His daughter Nicola told me years later of his "silver cord" experience. When near death from his wounds, he saw himself hovering above his body, attached by a silver cord. This gave him a belief in some form of life after death, and later he became interested in Eastern mysticism and reincarnation. Our mother had a similar experience when she was near death from pleurisy and saw her favorite brother, Rex, walking towards her. Rex had been killed during World War I. She thought he was coming to get her but "I was too strong," she said.

After the war, Kem published four or five novels and numerous short stories based on his war experiences. One of his books was turned into a movie. Whenever I met him, he was unfailingly charming and funny and kind. I never saw my brother angry.

We became estranged over his unwillingness or inability to help care for our mother after she returned to England when I married. From my perspective, it made sense for her to finally return to her native land. I had run out of ideas of how to help her and wanted to begin an independent life with my new husband. I believe Kem tried to be helpful, but he had a young family and was struggling financially, and Sylvia was not about to take on the role of mother-in-law or Granny. So once again, off she went, looking for somewhere to settle, living on the money from the sale of our Virginia house.

After his divorce from Gillian, Kem was finding it increasingly hard to earn a living. His writing did not earn him enough, and he finally turned to his other talent, cooking. He became a chef and *restaurateur* for some years, until a changed world and perhaps poor health pushed him onto the sidelines.

In 1994, when I finally set about trying to find Kem through the

British Red Cross, I was given the shocking news that he had died six years earlier of a heart attack. The counselor at the Red Cross tried to comfort me by telling me she had located his two children and would ask them if they were willing to be in touch with me. The same day, his son, Johny, called me on the phone. Later, I met both Johny and his older sister, Nicola, who has become a regular and loved presence in my life.

CHAPTER 21
Goodbye, England

In 1945, my brother, Kem, was demobbed from the Commandos and came to live with us in Hassocks. It turned into one of the coldest winters on record, and England was on its knees. Everything was still rationed except fish, which was plentiful now that the waters surrounding England were safe. Kem was trying to become a writer and spent his days typing on the dining room table.

This was the only room with a coal-burning stove, and we practically lived in it. There was no central heating, and limited fuel for heating water. The living room, with its large windows overlooking the garden, had only a fireplace. The bedrooms were freezing, and the small kitchen was warmed by the oven. Once a week we bathed in an inch of hot water in the icy bathroom.

My indulgences were chocolate and the movies. There was a cinema in our village where I used to walk to see Hollywood musicals. First I bought my week's chocolate ration and ate it in the movies. Once, my brother came to get me after the movie. He scolded me for ignoring my mother. I was angry with her for treating me like a child, not as an equal—the way she treated Kem.

I liked field hockey and riding my bicycle. Janine and I took horseback riding lessons. I learned how to adjust the saddle and bridle and how to mount the horse and hold the reins. I loved the feeling of the horse under me and the excitement of the gallop.

Soon, Kem left us to live with a family of writers who had set up a kind of commune during the war. Joan Grant, her husband, and her daughter, Gillian, provided the sympathetic family Kem had never known.

Joan Grant wrote stories about previous remembered lives and gathered around her people of like mind, who saw in her a wise woman and healer. She later married a psychiatrist, and together they started a practice. These were the glamorous people, I thought, and felt awed and attracted when Kem described their lives. They must have encouraged Kem's writing and provided a style of life that suited him, one that valued intellect and the arts over materialism and comfort. However, they had no interest in us, so Kem drifted away once again.

About this time, Jack Pratt's mother, June Mullaney, reentered our lives: the grandmother we had fled in a midnight taxi ride soon after arriving in America in June 1940. She and my mother must have patched up their quarrel. She tried to convince my mother to return to America, where she would find us a place to live with a good school system. She would undertake to support her granddaughter, Janine, which would benefit the three of us with housekeeping funds.

I was being a teenage pain in the neck, my brother had left, and food and fuel were very limited. Sometime during that extremely cold winter, the pipes upstairs burst and water came cascading down the staircase, then froze.

My mother grabbed the lifeline that June threw out. Her continuing presence in our lives was the price we had to pay for her much-needed management and support. Sylvia was simply not equipped to make a life for herself and two young girls. She was a war widow like many others but, instead of looking for work, she continued to inhabit the persona she forged for herself when she married Jack Pratt and accompanied him to southern Europe. I am sure she did not want to be an English housewife again and, even less, a working woman, certainly not a "shop-girl" or an "employee" as she called those who worked for others.

Her best qualities were endurance and cheerfulness. She learned to lower her expectations, to become thrifty and buy nothing but necessities. She became an enthusiastic and good cook using simple, basic ingredients. She would have made the right man a good wife.

Thus, about a year after we arrived in England, we re-immigrated to the United States, sponsored once again by our not-so-wicked grandmother. We packed up our belongings and had them shipped. This time, we sailed first class on the *Queen Mary*. What was my mother thinking? What I remember of the voyage is mainly the dining room, which was vast with multi-course dinners, most of which I didn't eat.

CHAPTER 22

1947: America Redux

In the summer of 1947, two years after we had left America to return Home, we once again arrived in New York City. This time, we made our way to Winchester, Virginia, the town June had selected for us because of its endowed public high school. No one ever accused June Mullaney of being stupid: self-serving, despotic, and often cruel, but not stupid. She must have gone to the library, where there would have been a public record of high schools around the country with their academic standing and resources. It was a great choice.

Thus, we closed the door on Europe and on the dream of returning that had kept my mother going during the lonely five years of war and eventual loss of her husband. She proved once again to be resilient and optimistic. Her taste for adventure was an advantage here, unlike later when it became a reflex reaction to discontent and uncertainty. While most people react to disaster by digging in their heels and turning their backs to the wind, my mother always took flight. But this time, this move engineered by our wise ogre of a grandmother was the best one we ever made. It gave us nearly 10 years of stability, protection, and nourishment. It saw me through my teenage years and beyond. The path was somewhat rockier for my sister who, more closely tied to her grandmother, paid a higher price. Whereas June had no interest in my upbringing, she was determined to fine-tune Janine's.

When we first arrived in Winchester, we stayed as paying guests

in the home of Nellie and Sandy Baker. Their house was modeled on
the Southern plantation, with white columns set on high ground above
Washington Street in the old residential section of town. During the
1950s and later, when my generation began to make money, old houses
like this one were snapped up by the new entrepreneurs who modern-
ized them. But just after the war when we arrived, prosperity was a
good 10 years away. Winchester was not badly off, as it had a regional
hospital that provided jobs and attracted professionals to the area, and
also a thriving apple business.

Nellie Baker, or "Miss Nellie" as she was known, was a small, dignified woman with white hair, a one-time beauty who welcomed us as
family. We had spent the war years in Savannah, after all, where she
had relatives and some of my mother's friends were known to her.
Sandy was a small thin man with a lock of graying hair falling over his
forehead and a perpetual cigarette between his fingers. He did not say
much.

The house was large, with many bedrooms—all poorly lit. Virginia
creeper, a kind of ivy that turns brilliant red in the fall, covered the
house and most of the windows. When electricity replaced gas, usually
only one electric outlet was provided per room, so modern fixtures and
lamps required extension cords. These increased over the years until
they festooned the rooms, running along the baseboards, looping over
the furniture.

My mother had agreed to let Janine live for a time with June in
France so she might attend a French school and continue with the
horseback riding she loved. When June arrived to collect her granddaughter, she was horrified by the possibility of fire. A Yankee, she was
used to less primitive electrical systems. She located the escape routes—
large windows far from the ground many with broken sashes that
would not open.

My private plan was to break the window and climb down the
vines for help, as Nancy Drew, girl detective, would have done.

Although we tried not to touch any of the wires, mild shocks were an everyday occurrence.

June had spent the war years at *Sunnytop,* her farm in New Hampshire where we had landed seven years before from Portugal, and whence had fled on that midnight taxi ride after Sylvia and June cataclysmically clashed over loyalties. Remember, our stepfather had hired a German nurse for his children in the '30s. I suspect he and his mother admired German culture, and some of that admiration lasted into the early war years. But a lot of dark water, both historic and personal, had flowed under the bridge. June was now a benefactor; her son was the devil.

We ate our meals with the family, cooked and served by Mary, the black maid. Miss Nellie treated her like a slave, beating her (it was rumored) when displeased. No one else entered the kitchen; it was a room of black encrusted pans—and cockroaches. When I found one in my stewed tomatoes, Mary took away the plate, removed it, then returned it to me.

Almost every family I knew had one house servant and a man who did yard work. Otherwise, the black population was invisible to the white world. It went to different schools, different stores in different parts of town. As newcomers from another, older world, we simply accepted what we found. We were welcomed as family members from the old country, and we, in turn, accepted and were grateful for the hospitality.

Years later, after I moved North, I realized how different things would have been for us if our language had not been English or if we had landed in some other part of the country. The North would not have been as welcoming, nor would the West or Midwest. Like a homing pigeon, my mother moved South during the war until she found Savannah. Our second attempt to find a home in America, aided by June's intelligence, was even more successful. This time, we found our English community in Virginia.

Through Nellie Baker, I met young people of my age—children of her friends and relatives—and they became my first friends. Some were aristocratic Southerners whose families had been planters in pre-Civil War days; all of them were connected to leaders of the community. This group of young people even had a name. They called themselves "The Crowd."

All of us were about 15, one year into high school. For many of these young people, high school was the cut-off between public education and preparatory school. Even Handley High, with its large endowment and high academic standing, did not fulfill the social or perhaps educational requirements for this privileged group. With one or two exceptions, all my friends were enrolled in private schools to prepare them for college. I was shocked and disappointed when I discovered none of my new friends were going to be my schoolmates. I was once again going to school with strangers.

My other, more profound problem was that the principal of Handley High school, Mr. Browning, would not give me credit for work I had done in England and insisted I enter the first year of high school—ninth grade. This put me a year behind my age-mates. I protested that I had been near the end of secondary school in England but he was unyielding. It was a matter of credits. I was angry and humiliated but in those days you did not argue with the principal.

John Handley High School was named for the judge who endowed it. An Irishman, he immigrated to Pennsylvania and made his fortune in the steel mills. Although he never lived in Winchester, he often visited close friends and is said to have felt a deep connection to the town. He gave a public library and an endowed public school system. These were the years before integration. Besides Handley High School, there was William Douglas high school for African-Americans as well as separate primary schools. These schools were built and are maintained today by public funds and the Handley bequest. "Barring some financial disaster, this fund will remain, as Judge Handley intended it to remain, as a perpetual contribution to the education of the children of Winchester." (Quarles, *John Handley and The Handley Bequests to Winchester, Virginia.*)

Handley High is a Greek Revival building with white Doric columns set on high ground, surrounded by green grass and shrubs, above the football field and surrounding neighborhood streets. Its generous endowment enabled the school to offer programs and hire teachers of a higher quality than many public schools. Those of us in the college-bound program were expected to take combinations of Latin, a modern language, algebra, geometry, general science, chemistry, physics, biology, numerous English courses, and a variety of other electives. I chose typing and shorthand, as I had one eye on earning a living as soon as possible. My other eye was kept firmly on what I loved: English literature.

For some months after we departed Nellie Baker's firetrap, we lived in a duplex on the extension of Loudoun or Main Street while we waited for our furniture to arrive from England. Across the street lived a family who became our friends. Irving O'Connell was Irish: a tall, large, white-haired man with a limp. His wife, Beatrice, had served in the Woman's Army Corps during the war, and had parked her two children with relatives for the duration. Little Bea, as her daughter was known, was beautiful, with the dark hair and white skin of the Irish. Her brother, Evan, was said to be highly intelligent and was away at school even as a child.

This family befriended us in very practical ways. Irving's profession as a contractor/plumber made him a lot of money. He liked my mother in the way that men always liked her. I don't think they actually had an affair, but he was always hanging around. He repaired the plumbing for us and fixed the broken switches. Beatrice, who did not seem to worry about the nature of her husband's interest, was also a friend. "A diamond in the rough" was Sylvia's characterization of Irving (like her brother-in-law, Harold, who heaved the tomato at my sister). She believed Beatrice had married beneath her (like her own sister, Jesse), but she never discouraged Irving's interest.

Little Bea became the wife of the poet Theodore Roethke, her teacher in college. The wedding was across the street. Our hosts served mint juleps, a Southern tradition. Disappointed because there seemed to be no bourbon in my silver goblet of ice, sugar syrup, and mint, I complained to Irving, who was always teasing me. He frowned the way he had done when he caught me reading one of Frank Yerby's bodice-rippers, disguised as a historical novel. Not having a resident father, I did not recognize the protective impulse. I thought he was being critical or, worse, treating me like a child.

Theodore Roethke was a known drunk as well as a known poet. Little Bea was required (according to her mother) to bring him whiskey before he could get out of bed in the morning. Beatrice and my mother mourned the fate of this beautiful young girl in the thrall of an old goat, even if a famous poet. Drunk at his wedding, he danced with all the women in turn, taking each one in his arms for a spin. He could not read them his poems, so he danced with them instead.

Slim volumes of his poems had been placed on a small table in the corner of the room. I watched someone pick up one of these and turn it over without opening it as if it were a shard of ancient pottery: a mysterious object from another world. When I started reading and writing poetry, I found his poems generous and accessible in a way that poetry often was not. Later, I studied poetry at Syracuse University with Tess Gallagher, one of his students,.

My mother started looking for a house to buy and settled on one in the country on the main road to Berryville, a small, historic town where many old families owned property. They all had cars, of course. We had had no car since my mother's minor accident with the milk truck. What would happen to you, she said, if something happened to me? I have spent a lot of time asking myself that question. The possibilities, unthinkable at the time, later seemed almost sensible. I would have been sent to England to live with my father, and Janine would have been brought up by June, as was Jack's daughter by his first wife.

I suppose this imagined scenario is a version of the kidnapped-by-fairies or adopted-child story: alternative lives imagined—or wished for—by dissatisfied children with active imaginations. My sister would have been worse off, as June was a proven tyrant, intolerant of dissent—as Janine discovered when she dropped out of college. I would have lived with a stepmother and sister in postwar England, but I would probably have been educated and trained as a teacher. I would also have known my brother. I believe this would have been good for me. As it was, Mummy, Janine, and I struggled to keep our rudderless boat afloat.

The house was new and small, another brick bungalow similar to the one in Savannah. Set back from the main road on a plot of treeless and rocky terrain, it must have seemed private and manageable to a single woman with two children. Perhaps the house triggered happy memories. There were small grocery stores that still delivered to your house, and my mother's new friends all agreed to come and carry her to town for bridge and luncheons. I would be dependent on the bus for getting back and forth to school, as would my sister when she returned from France.

Our furniture arrived from England in crates. In one crate, we discovered a mouse that had somehow survived the trip. Mummy nurtured the mouse as she had nurtured the squirrels we brought home in Savannah. It was an English mouse after all, a fellow creature, far from home. Soon, however, the mouse made friends with local mice, and a new family of international mice appeared. Finally, traps were bought and set. The mice either died or fled to the wild.

Meanwhile, I entered the ninth grade at Handley High with a huge chip on my shoulder. Once school began, I very quickly became a star of the English classes, since I read everything long before it was due for class. Grammar was a bore, I thought, but providentially 10th grade was devoted to it and, combined with my appetite for books, I became a competent writer and excellent speller. One year, I even won the essay prize.

At first I would have little to do with my classmates, all of whom were a year or so younger. I continued to hang out with my new friends on weekends and soon started dating somewhat older boys, some in high school, some already out of school and working. Mainly, I was a sponge, soaking up everything that would help me grow up. I had no way of discriminating what would suit me, so I did a lot of discarding along the way. This did not seem a problem at the time. For all my reading, I did not acquire any real ethical sense until later. Hunger drove me: for experience, acceptance, and pleasure. I certainly did not know what I liked or what I could do, but I was trying to find out. Fortunately for me, the culture in which I was living was extremely protective of smart, pretty white girls.

It has become an accepted belief in our democracy that money equals class standing. This was not always the case. Genteel poverty and its pretensions have been with us as long as outrageous poverty. Tennessee Williams wrote about it in *The Glass Menagerie* and *A Streetcar Named Desire* in the mid-20th century and more recently we have seen *Grey Gardens*, the documentary, and later the musical, about the impoverished relatives of Jackie Kennedy Onassis.

I continued to see members of The Crowd, who were one or two years ahead of me in school. I also cultivated a friendship with the daughter of the principal, a tall, shy girl with few friends. She was older than I was, but this did not seem to matter. I often went to her house after school and spent the night or the weekend. This soon began to anger my mother, who thought I should come home. She called me selfish. She was right. I did not care. I hated living outside town in a small, new house on a rocky hillside: that was not the old Winchester I had fallen in love with, the one covered in Virginia creeper.

The next summer, June returned from France with Janine. I had been invited to a party by one of The Crowd but had no party dress. June, having spent years in the fashion industry, set to work making me a dress from an old one of hers. It was pink taffeta with puffy sleeves and probably a sash. This was my first dancing party, so I had no idea what was the right thing to wear. I had taken dancing lessons during the war when we lived in Hendersonville but had probably not danced since. I must have been very nervous but determined.

Someone picked me up, or perhaps June drove me in her red convertible. I remember the song "Red Silk Stockings and Green Perfume" playing on the jukebox, a favorite of the hostess. My dress was different from anything the other girls were wearing. Some of them were black strapless, and none of them were pink with puffed sleeves. I resolved never to make that mistake again. From then on, I chose my own clothes.

Afterwards, I went back to being miserable. My sister's presence did not seem to matter. She was four years younger and pleased to be back with her mother and sister. We had acquired a large black-and-white dog named Peggy, who became her friend and companion. I was not interested in Peggy or my sister, for that matter. I wanted only to be at school and with my friends. Most of all, I wanted to live in town where I could go to the movies and meet my friends at the drugstore. I was trying to grow up. Adolescence was not a recognized period of life in those days. You were a child or an adult. The passage between was a minefield no adult wanted to contemplate.

While we were living on the Berryville Road, I had my first boyfriend, Bob—probably an eleventh grader, two years older than I was. It was common practice for boys to date younger girls. He would come for me in his car or with another couple, and we would go to a school function or to one of the many roadhouses to drink and dance to music from the jukebox. I do not remember alcohol being part of the evening, but he might have drunk 3.2 beer, the only alcohol for sale. The alternative was to bring your own bottle, available at the state-run liquor stores. At the end of the evening, we would certainly have spent some time in the car kissing. When I conjure up Bob's face, I see him in kissing mode. No other memories have survived.

One day, I was waiting by the road for the bus to town. A car pulled onto the shoulder not far from where I was standing. I thought someone was going to offer me a ride so I started walking toward it. The driver's door opened to reveal a man, his fly open, his penis sticking out. I turned and quickly walked away from the car back toward my house. When I turned and looked back, the car had gone.

The bus was late that day, and all the classroom doors were closed when I got to school. I walked on the polished floors through the empty halls. I felt strange, as if some part of me had been replaced or removed.

I don't remember if I ever told my mother—probably not. I did not tell her things until much later, after I had gained control of my life, and then very selectively. I knew she would have been shocked. It didn't occur to me that it might have hastened our move into town. I thought she was from another world, disconnected from the one I was trying to become part of. I knew I had to be nice to her, but I would never have asked her for advice. I did not think she knew anything useful and felt I no longer needed her.

As a child during the war, I had been very dependent, afraid to stay away from home overnight. Within a couple of years this changed. My mother implicitly and explicitly compared America to the Europe she knew before the war.

"But, of course, I'm an outsider." This was her mantra, exempting her from all responsibility for opinions. She professed to like young people who, I think, saw her as sophisticated and sympathetic, like the characters in the movies. But I knew I did not want to be like her. I wanted to be an American.

CHAPTER 23

1947: Winchester

It must have been during the summer at the end of our first year that we sold the house on the road to Berryville and bought another house in the old part of Winchester, on Cork Street, near the hospital. This house was built early in the history of Winchester and was reputed to have served as a hideout for Confederate soldiers during the Civil War. The front door opened onto the brick sidewalk, with no front yard or porch. The floor boards were wide and sloping in the way of old houses, and some of the ceilings were not quite straight. The dining room was filled with the same heavy, dark furniture that had been in Mont'Alegre. The effect was Old World. We did not use this room much, but I liked it, as I liked the living room with the comfortable sofa and French side chairs and library table. I had lived with these things most of my life; they were familiar and comforting. They came with us wherever we went and settled wherever we put them. I liked that.

There was a staircase leading up from the front of the house; another, from the back, was designed for the maid. For perhaps a year or more, we had the whole house to ourselves with a bedroom upstairs each and, out back, a tiny postage-stamp garden around which my mother built a brick wall. As we had no car, the location was perfect. We could walk to school and into town. Sometimes (rarely) I would meet my mother out doing an errand or visiting a friend and always found it surprising, even mildly distressing, that she should be outside the house. It was as if I had come upon the sofa or dining room table inexplicably in the street.

These were my mother's best days. Five feet four with an hourglass figure, her dark hair streaked with gray in a neat roll, she was still healthy and vibrant. Every morning, she dressed and made herself up and remained that way for the rest of the day. I never saw her in her nightgown or dressing gown after breakfast unless she was ill. A fast and vigorous walker, she stepped with agility over the uneven sidewalks; many of the bricks were heaved by the roots of trees, making the surface treacherous. I turned my ankles so often, they became weak and swollen. Doctors were not in our budget, so I consulted a library book on ankle exercises and after some time, my ankles were again strong.

My mother remained optimistic and cheerful in spite of her financial problems, interested in the affairs of the world. In the '50s, she listened to all the McCarthy hearings on the radio, expressing aloud her disapproval of Joe and his lies. She liked to read and had at one time been a fan of Khalil Gibran and his book *The Prophet*. She read some novels and liked adventure and exploration. She regretted her lack of education, often telling me that they were taught nothing in the school she attended as a girl. She would like to have read Milton and Keats (she owned copies of their poems) but felt inadequate to understand them.

My sister and I had mothers as different as our fathers, even though they were one and the same woman. My mother was educated in the restricted way of her time and worse, possessed of a set of attitudes that doomed her to believe she was incompetent. Men ruled her world. They were superior beings, if not by nature, then by fact. But while my mother was warm and irrepressibly cheerful, my sister's mother was artificial and bitter and, worse, disappointed in her younger daughter.

Sylvia never contemplated remarriage, perhaps because no one turned up. She was different from other women. She certainly had lovers, mostly after she returned to Europe, though not while we lived

Janine Pratt, age 15

in Virginia, as far as I know. Perhaps she did not remarry because she preferred her single state, with all its privations and insecurity. I do not think being alone was hard for her, although she used to say she missed having a man in her bed. She learned to live on very little.

Winchester in the late 1940s and '50s was a protected backwater; people were still licking their war wounds, the turbulent future only glimpsed. Rock 'n' roll had not yet come to our attention. The birth control pill had not been developed, and diaphragms were fitted by doctors only on engaged or married women. There was a kind of stasis to life that was both unreal and deeply comforting.

In the house behind us, one of my friends from The Crowd, Kitty, lived with her sister, Pat, and their parents in the second-floor apartment of a large Victorian house owned by their step-grandmother, who lived on the first floor. Their mother was the daughter of her deceased husband's first marriage. Relations between the floors were tolerant if imperfect. Their father, a veteran, old and ailing, was caretaker of his wife, who periodically had psychotic episodes. At these times, she would go into town and run up large bills at the local stores and sometimes take off her clothes on Main Street. Someone would bring her home and the ambulance would be called to take her to the state psychiatric institution, where shock therapy was administered. After a period of time, she came home and lived quietly until the next episode.

Later, I wondered if our fractured families were the bond that brought us together. I was drawn to Kitty in part because of her beautiful singing voice and dramatic temperament. She was slightly exotic in a way most of the girls were not. She took voice lessons and was often a soloist in the church choir. Both sisters were interested in the theater and music. I loved musical comedy and really learned about it for the first time from my two neighbors. Music was always playing in their apartment particularly light opera like Menotti's *The Medium* and *Lost in the Stars* by Kurt Weill.

This was a new world for me, and I took to it immediately. It was an extension of the movies I had loved, like *Singing in the Rain*, *Gilda*, and *Cover Girl*. Perhaps because there were no demanding adults (the parents almost never came out of their room), their apartment was a haven where we said and did what we liked. Kitty seemed to have few household duties: someone cleaned for them, and their laundry was sent out. I loved the clean, pressed clothes when they arrived, so different from our own attempts to keep ourselves clean and ironed. My mother did send out the sheets but we had to move the top sheet to the bottom every two weeks, with a fresh sheet on top, thus saving on our laundry bill. The rest of our clothes we washed by hand or occasionally had dry-cleaned.

While my passion was books, Kitty's was music, which I did not know much about. It is hard to overestimate the importance of books for someone like myself. Our many moves from one country to another, loss of family, especially a father, and the need to adapt to different schools and people made me dependent on their stability. They were my guides, teachers, and entertainment, and they did not change. I lived in books more profoundly than I lived in the world. I knew I was lucky to have this world and recognized that I knew a great deal more than my friends, making me older in certain ways. What I only realized years later was how poorly prepared I was to live in the real world, which I thought was like the world of books. It was years before I understood that books are written from the perspective of one person. They do not represent the unpredictable and chaotic world we live in. All this book experience made me seem worldlier than my peers and—because I was also pretty—mysterious and attractive. Years later when the boy I loved in high school told me I was looking for a knight on a white horse, he was onto something.

I had found the public library, a copper-domed beauty, when we first came to Winchester, before our brief sojourn on the Berryville Road. I prowled the open stacks and discovered the writers I came to love: Somerset Maugham, J.B. Priestly, Graham Greene, Ernest Hemingway, F. Scott Fitzgerald, and many more. I did not read many women writers. This was not by design. There were not as many women writers. It was a time before television, cell phones, or disposable income. Books were my classroom, my friends, and my mentors. They probably saved my life, or at least preserved my sanity.

Besides novels, I read how-to books on anything I needed to know (like how to fix a weak ankle). I learned, for example, the connection between what you ate and how you looked. I wanted to be thin and shapely, so I stopped eating my mother's carbohydrate-laden foods like pancakes and bread dipped in bacon fat. I also stopped eating dessert. This, of course, led to endless conflict with my mother, who believed it was her duty to produce a sweet at the end of a meal and ours to eat it. She made the glorious Victorian desserts from *Mrs. Beaton's Book of Household Management* that she had grown up on: treacle tart, steamed pudding with hot golden syrup, mince pie, and lemon curd tart. I loved them all, but began a lifelong habit of denial in order to achieve and maintain a svelte figure. Fortunately, I was becoming a swan as well as excelling at school, so she stifled her complaints as she watched me go about my business of self-improvement.

She seemed to have no intuition about the transformation of child into adult. Perhaps she shared this with most adults of the time. Girls were encouraged to make themselves as pretty and agreeable as possible. Boys, of course, were expected to accomplish a great deal more. If there had to be a motto of the 1950s, it would have been DON'T ROCK THE BOAT.

Meanwhile, my last two years of high school were mostly wonderful. I was now part of my high school group in the academic program heading for college (even though I was not planning to go), as well as part of the larger group of The Crowd who came home from college on holidays and occasional weekends. Then we would go out dancing or to a party, usually to celebrate a wedding somewhere in Clarke County (richer and more prestigious than our own Frederick County). People identified themselves by their county, not by the town in which they lived, except for those of us who lived in Winchester, which was the largest town in our area. This identity by county, not town, still exists in the South, maybe because there are fewer large cities or because many people live outside city boundaries.

I modeled my social behavior on the girls I thought the most attractive and popular. By this time, the chip had fallen off my shoulder, and I loved school, especially English, and had no difficulty getting above-average grades in everything except math. The academic English course was taught by Edith Garrabrandt, who took her job very seriously and was seen as something of a terror. She felt a real responsibility to prepare her students for college, particularly in 12th-grade English. We read Shakespeare and the Romantic poets and George Eliot and Willa Cather, among others. There was a special section of 12th-grade English taught by our school superintendent, Garland Quarles, on *Hamlet.*

In 11th grade, before the pressure was on to prepare for college, Mrs. Garrabrandt taught English to whoever enrolled, including popular members of the football team. We were studying plural nouns.

"If you had to mail order for more than one mongoose, what would you ask for, Manuel?" asked Mrs. Garrabrandt.

"I would write two letters," replied Manuel.

The class broke up and even our usually stern teacher, who draped herself over the lectern revealing underwear straps when her blouse slipped off a bony shoulder. As she righted herself, all the while making a point, she hitched up her blouse to cover the straps. We loved her. She made us feel privileged and confident. My only career goal was to teach English in high school, although at the time it seemed impossible. Many years later, when I did go to college, I trained to become a high school English teacher, but by the time I was credentialed, there were no jobs. But that is another story.

I joined the drama club as a "prose reader," part of Public Speaking, which included debate. These extra-curricular activities were designed to round us out beyond academics, much like deportment and elocution for previous generations. As a member of the drama club, I tried out for and got the part of the mother in the senior play. I was also voted "most dignified" for our yearbook. What kind of person gets voted "most dignified" and is the mother in the senior play? This is the same person who caroused on weekends dancing and drinking, and who got one boyfriend fired from his job, or so he said. It did not seem a very serious matter at the time, and I forgot about it until a few years ago when I visited him and his wife and he referred to the fact he was fired. *Oops,* I thought. No wonder he didn't want to be my escort for the Apple Blossom Festival.

I was also a member of the Booster Club, which was designed to support our football team and into which you had to be invited. Membership was a privilege, perhaps related to grade point averages, perhaps to something else: whom we want to be part of our group. It was also a way for girls to participate in sports, largely a male activity in those days—but as boosters, not players.

I worked every Saturday at a dress shop in downtown Winchester from nine in the morning until nine at night, for five dollars. In the summer, I worked there half a day during the week and all day Saturday. I was the only girl I knew who worked. Many of the boys worked after school and during the summer, usually on local construction jobs, which paid very well.

My work at the dress store paid for my clothes, which I bought at the store for a discount and usually on layaway. Clothes had become (after books) my greatest interest. I would select what I could afford when the new season's stock arrived, and by the time school started in the fall, I had usually paid them off, and my new wardrobe was ready. I could not, of course, afford cashmere sweaters or other pricey garments, but I chose what I liked and felt comfortably similar to my friends. We wore pleated plaid skirts with socks and either saddle shoes or loafers. We all put pennies in our loafers. There were high heels for dress—too high and often uncomfortable. For these, I waited for the sales at the end of the season and put my feet in the X-ray machines that showed the bones of your feet. Like so much that was bad for us, it was fun.

Downtown Winchester was an important place. We congregated at People's Drugstore after school, where we drank cokes and ate toasted brownies with a scoop of ice cream. We also smoked, asking each other for a penny to make up the 16 cents for a pack of cigarettes. We sat at the counter and flirted with our boyfriends and talked about our teachers and each other. Most of the grownups were friendly and watchful. Everyone knew everyone and their parents.

Harold Funk, a large flabby man in his 30s, wearing a shabby jacket and tie, used to walk in one door of the drugstore and out the other, holding his imaginary radio to his ear, talking, talking, talking in his own language. I knew he was harmless (everyone said so) but he frightened me.

On Sunday, I sang in the Episcopal Church choir and for a brief time taught Sunday school. I loved the choir; I could sing at the top of my voice and no one told me to stop. The best time was Christmas Eve, when I went with my friends to the candlelight service at midnight. There was always a party beforehand, and we arrived at church in a cloud of alcohol fumes, threatening the safety of the congregation as we fumbled to light our candles. We sang all the old hymns, loud and off-key, until we recessed on "O Come All Ye Faithful."

There were two ministers during my time there. The first one had visited my mother when we lived on the Berryville road. They sat together in the living room and drank tea. I think they were mildly romantic but I did not eavesdrop on them; I was too embarrassed. Our second minister was younger and very intense. The older ladies loved him. For reasons I have forgotten, he turned me against the church, or perhaps something else did and I associate it with his tenure. I remember thinking him a fraud. After high school, I never went regularly to church again and for years called myself an agnostic.

Earning money became top priority when, sometime during 11th grade, my mother's monthly alimony and child support check stopped coming. She tried to trace Jack Pratt through the bank and his former place of employment, Ingersoll-Rand, but nothing came of it. No one seemed to know where he was. His mother, June Mullaney, was not in touch with him (she said). He had, in fact, always disliked his mother, and when we were still a family, he used to put her letters in a drawer without opening them.

Much later, after our mother died, Janine wrote to the Veterans Administration for information on her father, and they sent her boxes of files. He had filed one medical claim after another. She learned so much from these files she was able to write a book (Janine Pratt Moden, *Black Pearls and Hollyhocks,* 2001). She also learned from her half-sister, Betty, Jack's first child with his first wife, the whereabouts of Jack's last child, the daughter of the Spanish spy, and arranged a meeting

What stood out for me in this welter of unexpected and not particularly welcome information was that June had always known Jack's whereabouts. What we also learned was that he had come to settle after the war in the Eastern part of the United States, not far from where we lived, where for a time he made a good living as a stock broker.

Looking at this from the long perspective of over 50 years, it does not seem strange that he would have had enough of supporting a second family for more than six years. He had another child by then, and we knew he had lost his job with Ingersoll-Rand. I suppose, like all divorced men, he had hoped Sylvia would remarry. She was by then 58 years old with two teenage girls.

So what to do? The wolf was snarling around the door. The chimney needed repair. Our friendly bank manager agreed to let her pay the interest on the mortgage without paying anything against the principal. Still, we needed more income. The house became our cash cow.

My mother's first attempt to bring in money was to inform the Winchester public school system that she had two rooms to rent to teachers. She would give them meals. My sister and I moved into what had been the maid's room at the top of the back stairs, leaving our two rooms available.

When I started 11th grade, two young teachers moved in with us. One became my typing teacher, the other taught primary school. They were to eat breakfast and dinner with us as part of their board.

My mother, being English and well brought up, made a good

impression on the paternalistic school system. Young female teachers were treated very much like college students of the day. The school assumed an *in loco parentis* attitude toward them. My mother was expected to behave as a kind of house mother. Nothing could have been more alien to her temperament. She didn't care what the young women did with their free time. She needed their money and tried to feed them well. This was the end of it, as far as she was concerned.

The first problem was the food. Sylvia's English cooking (straight out of *Mrs. Beaton's Book of Household Management*), with a heavy emphasis on carbohydrates and heavy puddings or tarts for dessert, was not what these young women were used to. They wanted meat and fresh vegetables and some nice light dessert. They were in the market for husbands and did not want to compromise their slender waists.

Being close to their age and perceived as mature for my age (most dignified, cast as mother in senior play), I became friends with them. I tried to explain about my mother and her English cooking, all the while agreeing and sympathizing. I was definitely on their side.

One night, the issue of cooking flew out the window when my mother had to summon the ambulance. The young primary school teacher had tried to abort a pregnancy herself. Blood was everywhere. The school authorities arrived, followed by her parents. She was sent home as soon as possible and the other teacher moved to new lodging. My mother was black-listed by the school system.

After this, the three of us moved into the back part of the house, where a small kitchen was constructed. A wall separated the two parts, leaving the large front part of the house intact and available to rent. Janine and I kept the bedroom at the top of the back stairs next to the bathroom, and Sylvia slept downstairs next to the new kitchen. Our living room now had a door onto the street.

The main part of our house was rented to a pleasant young couple with no children. Our finances did not allow us to repay the mortgage or make any home repairs, but with June's small contribution to

Janine's support, my father's tiny contribution, a portion of my salary, and the rent, we squeaked by.

Sylvia, 1950

CHAPTER 24

1950: High School

For all my interest in books and English class and drama and musical comedy, I spent every weekend in a social whirl. I dated boys who were in college, but I also had a high school boyfriend, Ronnie, who was on the football team and the president of our class. His father was the Presbyterian minister in town, and his church had a youth center that held dances on the weekends. We dated regularly during the school year. When my older friends came home on weekends and during the summer, I went out with them to parties and dances at the country club.

I think this all worked as well as it did because girls like me were not expected to have real sex with our boyfriends. The boys did not expect it, although they probably took their cues from the girl. What was quite clear was that your value was considerably reduced if you "gave in." There were other girls for that, ones they would never marry.

My memories of the last two years of high school are happy, in spite of anxiety over money. We lived in the present, and very much from hand to mouth. Occasional financial challenges would occur, like my invitation to be one of the two maids of honor to the queen of the Apple Blossom Festival.

For our small community, the annual Apple Blossom Festival was comparable to Mardi Gras in New Orleans. It attracted a lot of attention, making it a commercial bonanza for the local merchants. There were beauty pageants sponsored by the local service clubs, who

Sally and Ronnie, 1951

organized floats celebrating aspects of local culture: the apple business, the fire departments, the Lions Club and the Elks, Shenandoah Valley and Handley High School. Celebrities were invited to attend, and many showed up. The year I was a maid of honor, Secretary of State George Marshall was an honored guest. Gurie Lie, the daughter of Trygve Lie, the Secretary General of the United Nations, was queen. Van Johnson, the movie star, agreed to appear and let me cut off his tie as a souvenir for his nonexistent fan club. In later years, the singer Patsy Cline drove her pink Cadillac convertible in the parade.

Apple Blossom Festival, 1948

Apple Blossom Festival with Guri Lie (Queen) and George Marshall (Secretary of State),1951

Apple Blossom Festival with Van Johnson, 1950

The Maids of Honor and the Princesses were all required to wear long white dresses similar to bridal gowns. This was a considerable honor and it required buying a specified white dress for the occasion. This was beyond our means. In the end, a friend of my mother's stepped in and paid for the dress. There was a moment in the dress shop, as I whirled in front of the mirror, when I saw tears in the eyes of that sweet woman that jolted me from participant to observer. I knew why she cried.

As a member of the cast of that year's Festival, I was caught up in the social whirl of lunches and tea dances. My picture appeared in the paper. I got fan mail.

When I look at those photos, I do not see a happy girl. What was wrong? I remember being bored and vaguely disappointed. What had I expected that was not forthcoming? As Gertrude Stein famously said, "There was no 'there' there." My only attempt to step out of the lock-step rhythm of the event was to invite someone other than my regular boyfriend to be my escort. He declined, having already made other arrangements. My boyfriend never knew I had asked someone else, but it should have set off an alarm in some region of my brain. It did not, and I drifted further on the path to marriage.

I have always been drawn to books about the pioneer experience, about "strangers in a strange land." I took strength from these stories but also read them as survival manuals: how-to guides on what to do in unknown situations like sex. My mother talked a lot about her experiences with men, but they were romantic, not practical. She also got the connection between menstruation and pregnancy backward. She believed that a woman became pregnant if she had intercourse during menstruation.

I learned the essentials quickly (information was easily available at the library), but the tenor behind the information was something else. Yes, it was possible to prevent pregnancy (with luck), but the behavior was wrong. Only bad (undesirable) girls had sex before marriage, and if you became pregnant life as you knew it was over. I was terrified of becoming pregnant. Even the harmless necking and petting we did in the back seat of cars and in secluded places were warned against by the "authorities." Those pesky sperm could wiggle right through your underpants and find their way to your eggs. I became so frightened that I stopped menstruating and eventually went to a gynecologist. He asked me if I had any reason to think I was pregnant. No, I said, knowing this to be the truth, although my fear was what the fear of God must have been when people believed He could see their thoughts.

The doctor gave me a shot, saying it would start my period unless I was pregnant. Fortunately, it did, and that seemed to take care of my hysteria.

By the time, we were seniors in high school, most girls had steady boyfriends, many of whom were classmates but some older and in college or working in a local business. I was perhaps unusual because I had a steady high school boyfriend but also continued to date other boys when they came home from college. These boys took me to dances at the clubhouse in the summer and to roadside taverns, where we danced to the jukebox and drank 3.2 beer or whiskey bought at the state run liquor store and carried in a brown paper bag. I went to parties of a largely older crowd with them, to weddings and celebrations of the old Confederacy.

Ronnie's father was the Presbyterian minister in town, and his church allowed teenagers to dance and socialize in the church hall on weekends. Most of the local churches did not permit this.

We were in the same English Classes and both loved the books we read. Ronnie was not only an athlete but the best student in the class. We must have seemed a natural pair: both smart, good at school. He was clearly headed for a fine career of some kind. I was very pretty. There was no doubt we loved each other. We did all the things that high school students did together: took walks and talked and necked. We had almost-sex, enough to have caused the hysteria that led me to the doctor.

We knew each other's families probably better than we knew any other families. His sister was about the same age as my sister. His father, the minister, was beloved by his parishioners and seen as not only a good man but a natural man: someone you could talk to. His mother was very different. She had an elevated sense of herself both socially and intellectually. She was from an old Southern family, originally English, composed of many high-church members. She was well educated and considered herself a writer, having published small volumes of poems and short essays. She looked down on her husband socially, which caused friction in the family and a lot of hurt. Ronnie always allied himself with his father. Although I thought Ronnie's mother was pretentious, and he and I laughed at some of her ways, I liked his parents and they liked me. My mother said she would not have been ashamed to introduce them to her family.

So many things were taken for granted in that window of time lasting (for me) from about 1948 to 1955, when I married and left Winchester. I went from childhood to adulthood in those few years, and it felt good—so good that I was more confident than I should have been. Because I usually played by the rules—I did not see any reason not to—the surrounding adults thought I knew what I was doing.

The important issues were college and, eventually, marriage. I did not want to go to college when I finished high school. I certainly did not want to get married.

The reason for the first was simple but not exactly the one I gave out for public consumption. My mother had no money to pay for college. The thought of asking my father in England never occurred to me. Why not? He would have been the obvious person to turn to. Although I had not seen him since just after the war, we wrote to each other and exchanged Christmas and birthday presents.

The reason I did not want to go to college had to do not only with money but with what I knew about college from all my college-going friends. They had been preparing for this important event for a year or more. There were choices to be made, clothes to be chosen, name tags to be sewn on, luggage to be bought, room-mates to be met.

I knew I could have had a scholarship. I also knew that with a scholarship I'd have to work—probably wait on tables. And how would I have paid for the rest of it? And what about my mother?

So I said I did not want to go to college; I could read all the books and learn on my own. Also (I insisted) I did not want to take certain required courses, like math and science. I said all this and more with such sureness that my teachers and probably the guidance counselor left me alone after a while. The assumption in those days was that a girl like me would get married soon and college was really only a frill on the basic necessity of marriage and children. All this seemed to make sense and went on making sense until after I married and finally entered real adulthood to find myself ill equipped and totally confused about how to live.

Almost the only professional work available to women after World War II was nursing or teaching; that was the landscape of the '50s for girls of the middle and upper-middle professional class in the South. One of my friends, the valedictorian of our class, went to Cornell University and yet still trained to be a public school teacher.

I graduated from high school into secretarial work and, five years later, marriage. Like many other women of my generation, I entered the world of higher education and professional work after I married and had children. By then, the world had changed: women had gone off to war along with men and, when they came back, demanded more equality. Women became accepted in colleges as mature entries and trained as professionals in graduate or medical school.

My classmates on the academic track took their electives in subjects that would help them in college. When I chose to learn to type and take shorthand, I knew it would get me work in an office, rather than a clothing store.

With the benefit of hindsight and knowledge acquired over the 50 years that separate me from high school, I realize I was not as trapped as I believed. It wasn't only that I could have asked my father to contribute to my education (and I think he would have done this). What I lacked was confidence that anyone owed me anything. We had struggled alone since I was old enough to understand what it meant to be a family consisting of a woman and two small children in an unknown place. We had been taken in socially, but financially we were very much on our own. There were certainly those poorer than we were, but they often lived near family. We not only had we no income to speak of, but no one to advise us. If there were social agencies, we did not know about them, any more than we knew we were supposed to register annually as aliens at the local post office. In any case, my mother would not have taken what she would have seen as charity. It was unthinkable.

I had not seen my father, Bill Bennett, since we spent that year in England after the end of the war. When he arranged to contribute something to my support in the 1930s, Sylvia and Jack were in love and paid no attention to something as unimportant as Bill's child support. By the 1950s, the small prewar contribution must have become negligible. Sylvia, of course, would never have asked him for an increase, any more than, years later, she would have applied for a pension under the National Health and Assistance in England. She would have qualified as a British subject and as a pensioner (i.e., an old person) with no income, but it was never thought of. I was too young and clueless in such matters, and my brother thought as she did. They both believed, but would not have said, that it was beneath them.

My mother was in her late 50s by this time but looked a good 10 years younger. She still had her pale complexion and hourglass figure, and she wound her dark hair around her head in the fashion of the day. Her naturally easy manner was expressed in an English accent she could hide behind if the going got rough. She fit into the world of Southern gentility that was fast becoming extinct or changed beyond recognition. Her friends were older than most of my friends' mothers—their husbands had been in the war, and some had not come back. Some were wealthy, but old wealth was not so rich after the war. Soon the new rich would sweep the remains of the old society away and create something very different.

By the late 1940s, things looked superficially the same. It was a time of recuperation: families were coming to terms with their war losses and beginning to build their futures. There were veterans everywhere, particularly in high school, older than the other boys and very attractive to the girls. I remember couples standing around during recess and after school, smoking and necking in the bushes. These men, back from the war, were not interested in high school activities like sports; they just wanted to finish their degree and get on with their lives. Some of them were already married.

During our senior year, one of my classmates got pregnant. No one spoke of it as she got larger and larger, although she hid the fact for a long time. I was fascinated, terrified, and amazed at her composure. I knew this could happen to anyone and that it meant the end of school—and probably everything else. It is hard to understand now, in this much more tolerant time, how devastating the prospect of unmarried pregnancy was. Years later, I learned it was not so uncommon. Girls either survived an illegal abortion or died, married or gave the baby up: it was all shrouded in secrecy and fear.

This girl we'll call Ellie was tough-looking but pretty, with a wasp-waist and heavy thighs. She was one of the cheerleaders, and she continued to lead the cheers at the football games even after she was heavily strapped in beneath the thick cheerleader's sweater. No one said anything to anyone. It was so shocking that the only response was to pretend it didn't exist. Even our English teacher, Mrs. Garrabrandt, looked at Ellie angrily when they passed in the halls.

Two months or so before graduation, Ellie was absent for a time. She returned in time to graduate. Her picture appeared in the yearbook with everyone else's, and I remember seeing her at one of the class reunions many years later. She toughed it out and beat the system, or so it seemed.

I learned the truth after I graduated and was working full-time for the county health department as a clerk-typist. One of my jobs was to file the birth and death certificates, which were kept in our office. I looked her up and there it was: a stillbirth certificate for a baby boy. No father was named.

For young women of the time, sex and pregnancy were locked together in a way hard to imagine since the pill. For "nice" girls, sex before marriage was a moral issue, not only a physical one. It was possible, of course, to buy condoms, but they were believed to be not only unreliable but immoral. It was not just avoiding pregnancy that mattered but remaining chaste. This (and your reputation) became compromised once you "went all the way," even if your boyfriend swore secrecy.

I knew how girls got pregnant and how they didn't, but, even armed with information, I was terrified of the possibility. Knowing what not to do did not entirely banish what were partly irrational fears. I was afraid (like all "good" girls) of compromising my reputation even though I genuinely liked and trusted my boyfriends. Sex was a minefield where one false step could destroy you.

After acquiring secretarial skills, I worked during the summer in a law office. As I got older and more self-assured, my relationship with my mother improved. I no longer resented her and in fact felt obliged to care for her. I felt her poverty deeply and did not think I should do anything to further annoy or upset her. This turned me into a nicer person but came at great cost, as it included the belief I should not leave her to go to school.

During the last two years of high school, some of my older friends graduated from their prep schools and were attending college: Sweet Briar, Hollins, Mary Washington, Wellesley. The boys went mainly to the University of Virginia in Charlottesville. Hardly anyone was educated outside the South.

I heard about the book lists for summer reading, the clothes, the rules of living in a dormitory, and later the mixers with neighboring men's colleges and the *in loco parentis* rules that strictly enforced the hours students had to keep.

By then, I did not even want to go to college. I had convinced myself that it would be a waste of time. I wanted to work and learn what I wanted to learn in my own way. What either no one told me or I did not hear was the value of an education beyond its practical aspect. I could get an office job without a college degree. I do not remember there ever being any talk of careers. I think I would have heard it in college but in high school it was not a popular topic. The assumption, of course, was that we would all marry.

I'm sure most of the mothers of my friends had not attended college but in the 1950s, after the war, middle-class professional families
were sending their daughters to be educated. Since they did not really
expect to have careers, the purpose of the education was to make them
better wives and mothers, very much like the purpose of my mother's
education in the early 20th century. Like all my friends, I accepted the
values of the time and place. I was committed to being an autodidact,
although I did not know the term. I felt in no way inferior to my
friends; I just had no money.

Occasionally a crack would open into the realities behind our careful social manners. One Christmas I made soft felt slippers for all my
friends. I must have read how to do this in a magazine. I bought the
felt and cut out the slippers and stitched them together and wrapped
them in wrapping paper.

I had not imagined how they would be received. But it was clear
immediately that my friends were embarrassed—perhaps because they
had nothing for me but (I thought) by the poverty of the present. I
had blundered across the line into the family lives of my friends who
socialized with each other. They shared holidays, and the families gave
each other presents and entertained.

We engaged in none of this. I was invited to all the parties and
always had a date with someone's brother or friend from school or a
local boy. My mother never entertained, nor was she invited by any of
these families. She had friends—mostly older women, a few with husbands. They played bridge together, but otherwise my mother did not
go out. Occasionally, before we lost our income, she would give a small
party and make a European meal: a cheese fondue, perhaps.

I remember a group invited for a *Fondue Genevoise* with Gruyere
cheese and white wine that my mother had learned to make in Switzerland. We could not get imported cheese, so she must have used a
domestic Swiss. The guests included the president of our bank and his
wife and perhaps four others. They had no idea how to eat out of a

common pot, spearing a piece of bread and dunking it in the molten cheese. They took their plates back to their chairs and ate there rather than standing around the pot. There was a lot of laughter—the hot local wine, the rubbery cheese. They were kind people, and I am sure made my mother feel appreciated. But as usual, I wished we could have been like everyone else and served a proper American meal.

In 1951, I graduated, and suddenly high school was over. For our prom, held in the gymnasium and decorated with our class colors, we hired a second-rate Dixieland band, customary at the time. One of my friends' parents invited some of us for a steak dinner before the prom to fill our stomachs with protein before the evening of dancing and drinking, culminating in a sunrise breakfast at a popular restaurant I had often been to after our country club dances in the summer. They served wonderful eggs and bacon and grits and biscuits to exhausted and often drunk teenagers.

That summer I worked in the law office as a fledgling secretary. They were kind to me and offered me permanent work after the summer was over. However, I had decided to attend a secretarial college in Richmond, Virginia, in the fall. For this, I had written to my father in England and asked for the tuition. He complied, as he probably would have done had I asked for money for college.

I thought this extra training would get me a better job, and I think I also wanted to go somewhere like the rest of my friends who were off to college. Mine turned out to be a poor choice, leading to a dead-end, not opportunities in a wider world that I had hoped for.

CHAPTER 25
1951: Richmond

After high school, I moved to Richmond in an attempt to find a way forward that did not include college but, instead, secretarial work and a new and different adult world. Ronnie, my high school boyfriend, was going to Davidson College in North Carolina, a small college with high academic standing connected to the Presbyterian Church.

I moved into a boarding house, one of Richmond's many Victorian row houses dating back to the beginning of the 20th century. The ground floor, occupied by the landlady, included the dining room, kitchen, and living room. The smell of boiled cabbage greeted you inside the front door. The rooms on the first two floors were occupied by older people, mostly single.

I shared one of two rooms on the third and top floor with my old friend and neighbor, Kitty. The other room was occupied by two other single women. The bathroom was one floor down. Kitty was attending Richmond Polytechnic Institute as a voice major.

One of our suitemates was slightly older, a working woman coming off a messy divorce and bankruptcy. The other came from faraway Oakland, California, training to be an occupational therapist, an occupation I had never heard of. The four of us became friends.

We ate breakfast and dinner together in the dining room, cooked by our landlady. After we had finished, we passed our plates to be scraped and stacked before being carried to the kitchen. I found this heaping of scraps and bones repugnant. Except for my brief stay at Nellie Baker's, it was my first experience living with people other than my own family. At the time, I had no idea of becoming a writer and missed a golden opportunity to write about this captive group.

One evening, I left the front door unlocked when there had been rumors of a cat burglar in the neighborhood. I had gone out after work to meet Ronnie, who had come from Davidson to stay with his aunt Louise, a widow with one daughter. She could not have been more different from her sister, Ronnie's mother. Whereas Peggy was self-consciously refined, Louise was natural and outgoing.

When I returned to the boarding house, I was greeted by an angry landlady. The first- and second-floor tenants had cowered in their rooms as some unknown male, finding the front door unlocked, had clomped through the house, apparently looking for someone he believed lived there. Finding no one around (doors locked, no sounds), he clomped out again. My roommates on the top floor were unaware of the interloper. I apologized; I was abject and promised to be more careful. The landlady agreed to let me stay on probation.

In fact, a few months later I moved out into a small apartment I arranged to share with Kitty's sister, Pat, who was also trying Richmond out as an alternative to Winchester. Pat had given up drama school in New York City, believing she was not a good enough to earn her living as an actress and was not suited for such a precarious life. I liked the idea of sharing an apartment better than living in a boarding house, and I found Pat more congenial than her sister. The two were not on good terms, so I never really saw Kitty again after this; she moved away and eventually married. I felt I had betrayed her by choosing her sister, but this did not stop me.

Meanwhile, I went to work part-time in a luggage store while attending the secretarial school. The store was run by a man and his wife, Eulalie, a lively redhead who used to excuse herself to "shake the dew off my lily." I helped out in the office. Their other employee was a young man, a newlywed who had taken his bride to New York City for their honeymoon. There, they had something they called pizza pie. We stared at him, wide-eyed. No one had heard of pizza pie.

Soon, I had enough of the secretarial school, realizing I already knew how to type and take shorthand well enough. Bookkeeping was shakier, but I did not plan to take a job as a bookkeeper. I left the school after the first semester and found a full-time job with a life insurance company as secretary to the director. I discovered I could quickly transform initial chaos into meaningful tasks. My boss was nice to me and even invited me home to dinner, where his young wife produced an elaborate meal that involved shrimp, an almost unknown food to me at the time.

Perhaps the most interesting event of my year in Richmond was my brother's visit. Kem and his wife, Gillian, were spending some months in Hollywood, where he was writing a movie script based on his novel. When Gilli became pregnant, she decided she wanted to return to England to have the baby. On their way back to New York, they stopped in Winchester to visit our mother, and I took the bus home from Richmond to see them.

I had not seen Kem since we left England four years earlier, and I had never met Gilli. My feelings toward my brother were complicated: a mix of awe, admiration, and resentment. I did not know him well enough to know if I loved him, except that he was my brother and had always been nice to me. Like my mother, he was English; I was American.

He had brought my mother some expensive scented oils by Mary Chess, a fashionable perfumer. My mother loved luxuries of this kind and, of course, could not afford to buy them. It was a perfect present. He brought me an umbrella, which he had bought locally at one of the women's clothing stores. The umbrella had a bamboo handle and was, I thought, very elegant.

Kem was charming, kind, funny, and loving. He seemed an ideal man. My mother certainly thought he was and made no attempt to hide her love and admiration. They seemed to have a special connection with each other, even though they had not seen each other for years. They called each other "darling," a word you never heard in America at the time except in the movies. I had grown up without a father and had not known any mature men. The only men I knew were boys and, casually, my friends' fathers and occasionally a friend of my mother's. Kem was kind and attentive. He seemed to have much more experience than most Americans at the time. He, after all, had been in the war and lived in many parts of Europe. He was a writer and lived with other writers of diverse and complicated backgrounds. My overwhelming feeling was that I wanted to be the kind of person he would love and find attractive. I did not think I was worthy. I felt too young and ignorant.

He drove me back to Richmond after the weekend. He asked me where we should have lunch. I had never had a meal out anywhere, especially in Richmond, and was tongue-tied by the question. He spotted a Chinese restaurant, and we ate there. When he tried to kiss me goodbye I was too shy, and we ended by shaking hands.

I believe Kem would have liked to stay in California. The life would have suited him, and he might have done well as a writer. But Gilli wanted to go home. I did not see him again for about 15 years, by which time he had a second child with Gilli before they divorced, and had turned from writing to being a cook and restaurateur.

He could not make a living by writing. Money was always short, and he was still responsible for his children when their mother remarried. The restaurant business is very hard work as you age, and, as Kem became overweight and continued to smoke, making ends meet became difficult. As his children grew up, they helped him.

I wanted to become a writer because of him. I would have liked to be his friend.

At the end of my year in Richmond, I decided to move back to

Winchester. I could live at home, thereby giving my rent money to my mother and helping her out in other ways. Richmond had proved a disappointment; it had not provided anything really new or interesting for me, either socially or professionally. I realized that secretarial school was redundant; I had those skills. A fancy secretarial school like Katie Gibbs in Manhattan where the girls lived at the Barbizon was preferred by college graduates. It would have provided placement in desirable locations that hired desirable young men, but I could not afford the fees.

The year in Richmond had provided me with some new experiences, mostly those of living on my own and working in a new city. I had also been able to go to a couple of theater productions: Strauss's opera *Die Fledermaus* and a production of *His Eye Is on the Sparrow* with Julie Harris and Ethel Waters. I sat in the nose-bleed section of the second balcony and loved every moment of it. I had loved the theater for many years, even though I never aspired to act: I think I knew I was too self-conscious. Later, I tried my hand at writing a play, which I called *The Fourth Monkey.*

So it was home to Winchester. I felt I had abandoned my mother for a not very good reason. If it had led to a better job or some interesting new friends, the move would have felt justified. As it was, it seemed pointless. My decision to return felt responsible and grown-up. I found a good job in the local Health Department as a clerk-typist, which required secretarial skills. The pay was poor, but it was interesting work that taught me quite a bit about the population we served with our public health nurses, sanitation officers, and clinics. I liked it better than working for the insurance company.

My social life also improved, as I knew a lot of boys now in college and others who were working locally. Ronnie's parents had moved to Florida, so he no longer had a home to come back to but he hitchhiked many hours and slept on our sofa. Pat had also moved back to Winchester and was now engaged to marry a young lawyer in town. My sister was a high school student by then, and she also worked part time in a shoe store.

For a few years, life was stable, and not very different from my last year of high school. I was making more money and no longer had to work all day Saturday. I could sit in my open window, puffing on a cigarette, or lie on my bed and listen to the Saturday afternoon Metropolitan Opera broadcasts until I fell asleep.

By 1954, my mother had reached the end of her resources, and we knew that some change would have to be made. The bank wanted more return on its loan than the monthly interest, and the chimney was falling down. We were notified that we had to maintain the property or put it up for sale. My sister had not yet finished high school.

Ronnie and I decided to marry even though he had one more year of college. My mother could sell the house, and I would use the money my father gave me as a wedding present to buy her plane fare to England. There she could stay with Kem until some other arrangement could be made. Janine would live with Ronnie and me while she finished high school, after which her grandmother, June, would send her to college. All this came to pass over the next two years. Then our Virginia idyll came to an end, and we went out into the world.

CHAPTER 26

The World

The three things that happened to us in this new location seemed at first to have been the result of sensible, even wise, choices. Ronnie and I were married in the summer before his senior year in college. His father performed the ceremony in a small white Presbyterian church with box pews, dating back to before the Civil War. His uncle Frank gave me away, as I had no male relative in America, and in those days no one would have thought it proper for a mother to give away her daughter.

I engaged in the same wedding preparations as all my friends. Ronnie and I chose our silver and china patterns and listed them in the local store that specialized in fine china, crystal, and silver tableware. The presents that were delivered to our house seemed almost a miracle. My mother had never purchased china or silverware or linens in my lifetime. What we had was old and had had many years of use. I put these new beautiful objects out on the table as was the custom so that the guests who came to the reception could admire them.

To be sure we would have actual plates and cutlery for daily use, I had been saving coupons from the Kellogg's cereal packages. In those days, you could send the required coupons, add cash, and eventually acquire many place settings of silver plate, even monogrammed. I also bought bath towels and sheets from my savings. It all seemed normal and right, built on solid ground, not on the shifting sand of my childhood.

As a bride, I wore one of my mother's evening dresses from her prewar life with Jack. It was cream-colored, with inserts of lace. My sister, Janine, and Ronnie's sister, Mary, were bridesmaids, and one of Ronnie's friends was his best man. The scale of the wedding was small, as was the reception in our living room at home. In the photographs of Ronnie and me cutting the wedding cake, we look handsome and excited.

Afterwards, we drove in our old Plymouth to a small lodge somewhere in the Pocono Mountains, a modest resort in those days before there were heart-shaped beds. We put a towel on the bed before we lay down in order not to stain the bed sheet. We need not have worried. Whether it was my teenage horseback riding or some other athletic activity, there was no blood.

From there we moved to Davidson College, where Ronnie had rented an apartment for us—the second floor of a private home. There were not many married undergraduates in those days. I got a secretarial job in the college alumni office.

I remember being homesick. But I also remember the newness of living as a wife. Ronnie was busy being a student, and I was working, but I also had to do things like cook and, I suppose, clean. I remember the cooking but not the cleaning. We drove to the supermarket once a week where we bought our week's groceries for $10. We did not starve; we did not even go hungry. My small salary and some money Ronnie had saved from his summer work seemed to be sufficient. On Sunday mornings, our only day together, we lay in bed, making love and reading the paper.

When my in-laws came for Ronnie's graduation, I wanted to cook a picnic shoulder (we called it ham) but could not find a recipe. In the South, everyone knew how to cook a ham: it was like looking for instructions to boil an egg. But we had never cooked large pieces of meat, or much meat at all. I remember cutting the hard outer rind off the ham before scoring the fat and piercing it with canned pineapple, brown sugar, and cloves before putting it in the oven. Fortunately, all these small picnic shoulders were precooked as part of the chemical preparation. The real hams were hung and smoked prior to cooking.

I had eaten these in Winchester, but had no clue how they were prepared. My first ham (shoulder) was pretty tasty, and no one got sick, so I considered it a culinary success. Ronnie's father gave him a watch for graduation, which was a surprise to everyone, including his mother. Why didn't he tell me, she asked?

During the first year of our marriage, Ronnie had applied to the Graduate School of Psychology at Yale University and was accepted. We were going to New Haven. I had not been up North since I was a child in Jackson Heights.

We hired a U-Haul trailer for our few possessions and when school was over we set off for New Haven, following Route 1 through all the small towns and strip malls to the New England city of New Haven with its Green and white-steepled churches. Our apartment was a street away from the Green and a few blocks from the Institute of Human Relations, where Ronnie had his classes and where I worked as a secretary in the Child Studies Department.

It was in New Haven that I became a naturalized American. It was so easy in those days. I was married to an American and had spent and uninterrupted number of years in residence. The government forgave my failure to register annually at the post office: I blamed my mother, and the immigration officer nodded sympathetically.

Meanwhile, my mother had sold our house in Winchester, along with most of the contents, and had booked a flight to England. My sister, Janine, was going to live with us in New Haven and finish her last year of high school there before going on to college.

All this sounds rational. Why didn't it work better? With the benefit of 50 years plus hindsight, I believe it was because none of the three of us were doing what we wanted. We could not afford to do what we wanted so we followed a plan that suited no one.

My sister, Janine, entered an inner city school as a senior and learned very quickly that the only way to survive and get her diploma was to keep a very low profile. She had no friends; she went to class and came home. She had wanted to finish high school with her friends in Winchester, but no one had offered to take her in for her final year, so she had stoically fallen in with the plan. It is to her credit that she finished the year and graduated. She had decided on Duke University in North Carolina for college.

During her first year there, she met a boy, and they fell in love. He must have been in his final year, because they decided to marry, and Janine dropped out of college. She wanted a home of her own, she told me many years later. Her grandmother disowned her: stopped her allowance and removed her from her will. As we learned years ago, June Mullaney was smart but cruel.

The marriage produced three children and, eventually, divorce. Whatever regrets my sister had about leaving college and marrying, they did not include the children who she says provided her happiest moments.

Meanwhile, our mother had flown to England with a small nest egg from the sale of the house and its contents. It must have been very hard for her to part with the pieces of furniture and other objects she had acquired during her prewar life. For her, it was one more adjustment downward. She lived for a time with my brother and his wife and their two small children. Not surprisingly, the two women did not get along. Sylvia had not lived in someone else's house since she was young, and Kem's household, built around the needs of a writer and his family, was not a comfortable place for her. I am sure she was jealous of my brother's family and ill at ease without a place of her own. She moved out and became a wanderer for the last 20 years of her life, remaining in England for a time but then returning to Portugal. Her last home was Cascais, only a few miles up the coast from Estoril, where she had lived happily before the war.

During the next two years in New Haven, Ronnie studied for his Ph.D. in psychology, as well as working for one of the young professors in the department—a typical arrangement at the time that paid his tuition and provided a small stipend for living expenses.

I worked for a Viennese child psychologist, a follower of Freud and his psychoanalytic theory. Unlike all the other secretarial jobs I had held, this one required that I be part of a team, not just a hired hand. At first, this was flattering and intriguing. After a time, I realized that it was a kind of indoctrination. In order to satisfy Katie Wolfe, my boss, I had to reveal myself in ways I had not previously imagined. It was not that she wanted details of my private life, rather she expected a kind of intellectual openness that I had no previous experience with nor, at the time, any capacity for providing. I had no intellectual training beyond high school and whatever I taught myself by reading. After the initial feeling of admiration wore off, I felt frightened and bewildered. I tried to tough it out and behave as if I understood what was expected of me and how to contribute something. Finally, I resigned, after trying to explain to Katie why I did not want to work there. I no longer remember what reasons I gave except she listened to me and accepted my resignation. She probably understood more of what was happening to me than I did.

At the same time, I fell in love with one of the other graduate students. How could this happen only a little more than a year after Ronnie and I were married? It is probably the kind of thing that happens regularly to high school sweethearts when they go away to college. The comfortable cocoon we lived in during high school was somewhere else in another time. Ronnie was working hard at his profession; I was in free-fall. I did not even have a home to retreat to for advice or, at least, refuge.

For a time, I survived by finding another job in another department, a job that required organizational skills and more independence than my previous one. This provided a lifeline for a time. Meanwhile, my lover and I met when we could and lived from day to day. He was married with two children. I started seeing a psychotherapist, who I believed kept me out of the hospital but provided almost no other help

of any kind. It was during the period when therapists did not say anything; they simply listened. I badly need some sort of advice.

Finally, towards the end of our second year in New Haven, I could
not stand the pressure any longer and told Ronnie I thought we should
separate. I told him about the affair. He had accepted an internship
for the following year at a hospital in Chicago as part of his training.
I believe if I had had anywhere else to go, we would have separated.
He would have gone to Chicago without me.

This did not happen. We decided to go to Chicago together and
try again. At the time, I believed this had all been a kind of growing
experience that would produce a more adult me, that I would be able
to love my husband as I wanted to and that we would be able to continue a life together. We spent a year in Chicago, then back to New
Haven where our son was born and Ronnie wrote his dissertation.
From there, we moved to the University of Iowa in Iowa City for his
first job. I took courses in the English department and the creative
writing program. Four years later, our daughter was born.

But you could have had anyone you wanted, my mother cried
when I told her I was going to be divorced. That was certainly not
true, but it was true that I did choose Ronnie and not because there
was no one else around. I needed safety. He made me feel safe, and
then that was not enough. He was the smartest boy I knew, and I
needed smart. Perhaps we were just too young and unformed. He
deserved a whole heart, which I was unable to give.

University towns are good places for immigrants: many of us are
drawn to places of learning where our family and place of origin are
unimportant. It felt like home. It was here that I met the man I would
marry and live with for the next 45 years, most of them in a university
town or in Europe and Africa. Now we live on a small island off the
coast of Massachusetts. The same ocean that laps our beach laps the
shores of England and Portugal. This does not make me less of an
immigrant; it reminds me of who I am.

AFTERWORD

After our mother left Portugal in June 1940 with me and my sister, Janine, Jack remained behind in Lisbon to continue his work with Ingersoll-Rand. What we did not know until years later, was that he also worked with the OSS, Office of Special Services, forerunner of the CIA. My sister learned years later that he successfully arranged for Jews to escape from occupied France into neutral Portugal. After the war, France awarded him the Legion of Honor for his work.

Since the end of World War II, all the countries that remained neutral, joining neither the Allies nor the Axis powers, have been severely criticized and some prosecuted for the part they played in persecuting the Jews. All of them sold raw materials such as wolfram to Germany for use in making arms and munitions. Many of them, including Portugal, stored Nazi gold, stolen from refugees and the inmates of the concentration camps. This aspect of the conflict was not widely known until years after the war ended, including the full extent of Switzerland's involvement.

During World War II, Portugal was a conduit for Jews escaping occupied France, Belgium, and the Netherlands. They had to find their way across Spain, a fascist country, over the mountains into Portugal. There were heroes like the consul general in Bordeaux, Aristides de Sousa Mendes, who defied Salazar's decree to deny Jews entrance into Portugal. In three nights he issued 30,000 visas. He was later fired from his job and died penniless.

The Germans never invaded the Iberian Peninsula, and Lisbon and Estoril became hotbeds of spies and refugees. The shops were full of luxuries and the Palace Hotel and casino in Estoril welcomed rich and aristocratic Europeans. The Parque Hotel was a center of the German propaganda machine, busily making future business contacts. Meanwhile, charities in Lisbon were helping refugees who were being fleeced of whatever they brought with them to secure passage out.

It was in this atmosphere of excitement, intrigue, and terror that Jack met a Spanish aristocrat and spy who had been working in France when she was discovered and was able to leave France only because her cousin was king of Spain. She then went to work for Jack and the OSS. One thing led to another, and they started living together. She must have been in the photos Jack sent to us in Savannah: a group of young people enjoying a picnic.

Jack Pratt, handsome look-alike for Clark Gable: intelligent, brave, charming, resourceful, and definitely not a stay-at-home Dad, must have had a helluva war. Afterwards, he and his new family, including another baby girl, lived well in America and Europe until his fortunes ground to a halt and he declared bankruptcy. His mother, whom he despised, was always nearby, offering help along with unwanted advice. We knew none of this and believed he was lost somewhere in the postwar world. Not a bit of it. June knew where he was at all times but never revealed his whereabouts to us or to our lawyer.

APPENDIX

Transcribed from a copy of the original letter written to my father, William Deverell Bennett, from his father, James William Bennett, dated July 6, 1933:

I will write from myself so you will know to think of them as generations older than yourself.

For instance: My grandfather, William Bennett (your great-grandfather) was an Indigo Dyer in the West of England and was brought over to Leeds by "Sheepshanks," a founder of the cloth Industry in Leeds and developed largely by him.

Grandfather settled down in Kirkstall near Sheepshank Mills and I think he and Grandma and their children must have been induced to come to Yorkshire about 1835 or near. Mother used to tell me how they related about the journey in a carrier's cart with their young children (no railways available then). He brought up Uncle Sam and Uncle William to be Indigo Dyers and father also, but father gave it up and went into the manufacture of cloth and did well until the Germans put on such duties as to kill the manufacturers who were in connection with this.

I was sent to Germany age 17 for 16 months to learn German in making cloths for Germany. (Pilots and other plain cloths I believe were cotton warps.)

Well, Uncle Sam started for himself at Horbury and did well. His son George carried on; I believe the business is still in the Indigo Dyers Association.

Uncle William was a clever Indigo Dyer and had some fine chances of being employed by leading firms but he never kept his jobs. He was a wanderer and was often restlessly shifting about. He had a son who went to America and at one time was Mayor of Chicago.

Well, I must return to Grandfather Bennett who died when about 76 (I think). He had the honor of gaining the FIRST Diploma for Indigo Dyeing at the first Exhibition ever held. I think it was in the early (eighteen) fifties and in Hyde Park. The building was moved to Sydenham and is now the Crystal Palace near us.

The family was located in Gloucestershire amongst the West of England Cloth Mills. These were founded by the Huguenots, as you know, in the previous (18th) century. Grandfather William Bennett married into the Deverell family, one of them was a great and good lady known in the District for good works. I suppose Grandma was a daughter, being a Miss Deverell. (They must have married between 1820 and 1825 when he would have been in a position to marry. His father had trained him for at least ten to twelve years. They had six children.) We called my second son, William Deverell (Bill), after them.

I should like to mention that I remember my father's cousin, Jim Paton, dead many years, who came from the same district and was about Father's age. He was established in London as a cloth finisher: the firm was Nicole & Paton, the former still in existence. I saw their cart the other day in the City. Father used to tell us of wonderfully strong deeds done at "Mount Vernon" where they lived. One was the wheeling of a tremendous load in a wheelbarrow up a fearful hill there. I cannot recollect if it was one of the family; I think so, as he was very proud of it! They were all big men except Grandfather, only medium. Father and Uncle William were over six feet: hefty chaps.

The rough notes I make are actually from my father and his cousin so we can claim to carry the family history back to the Huguenots (who) settled in Gloucestershire.

William Bennett proceeded to Leeds with his family [in] 1835 as a Master Indigo Dyer, being called there by William Sheepshanks.

I remember Grandma always called him Ben-*nit* not *Ben*-nit as pronounced now. They [women?] called their husbands by their surnames."

Signed Jas Bennett 6/7/1933, born 1855.

REFERENCES

Anderson, James M., *The History of Portugal.* Westport, CT: Greenwood Press, 2000.

Livermore, H. V., *A New History of Portugal.* London: Cambridge University Press, 1966.

Quarles, Garland, *John Handley and the Handley Bequests to Winchester, Virginia.* Winchester, VA: Quarles, 1969.

ACKNOWLEDGEMENTS

I want to thank my sister, Janine Moden, for sharing the information regarding her father, Jack Pratt and my sister, Anne Gisburn for information about and photographs of our father, William D. Bennett, and his family. I am also grateful to Kim Chang and Tom Protisto for her help in editing and his with photographs. Last but not least, thanks and my love go to Nicola Bennett, my niece, who read and commented on the manuscript.